E S T A T E   P U B L [I C A T I O N S]

HUNTINGDON · S[T]

ST IVES   GODMANCHESTER

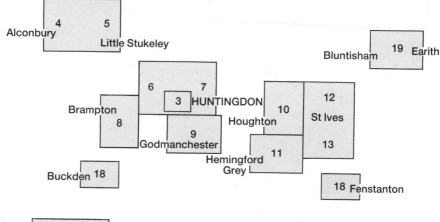

Alconbury 4 5
Little Stukeley

Bluntisham 19 Earith

Brampton 6 7
3 HUNTINGDON
8
Houghton 10
St Ives 12
9
Godmanchester
Hemingford 11 13
Grey

Buckden 18

18 Fenstanton

Eaton Ford 14 15
3
Eaton
Socon 16 17
ST NEOTS

Every effort has been made to verify the accuracy of information in this book but the publishers cannot accept responsibility for expense or loss caused by an error or omission. Information that will be of assistance to the user of the maps will be welcomed.

The representation on these maps of a road, track or path is no evidence of the existence of a right of way.

Car Park	P
Public Convenience	C
Place of Worship	+
One-way Street	→
Pedestrianized	▨
Post Office	●

Scale of street plans 4 inches to 1 mile
Unless otherwise stated

Street plans prepared and published by ESTATE PUBLICATIONS, Bridewell House, TENTERDEN, KENT.
The Publishers acknowledge the co-operation of the local authorities
of towns represented in this atlas.

Ordnance Survey® This product includes mapping data licensed from Ordnance Survey® with the permission of the Controller of Her Majesty's Stationery Office.

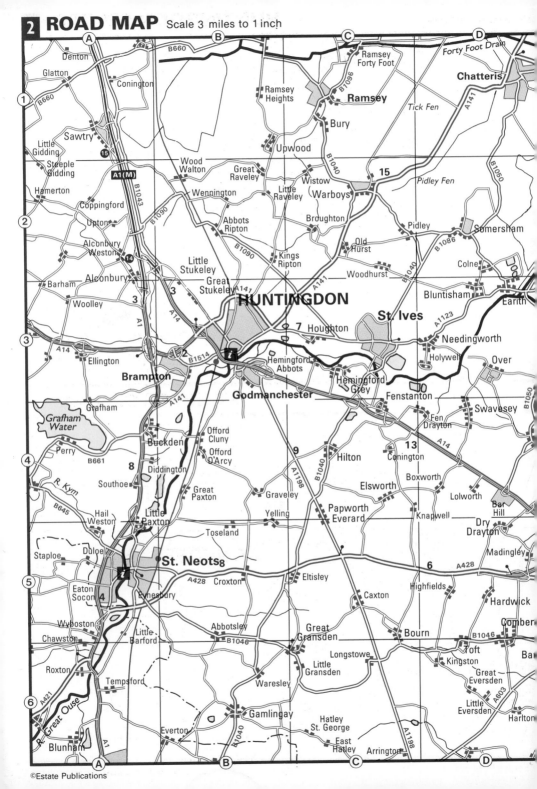

Scale: 8 inches to 1 mile

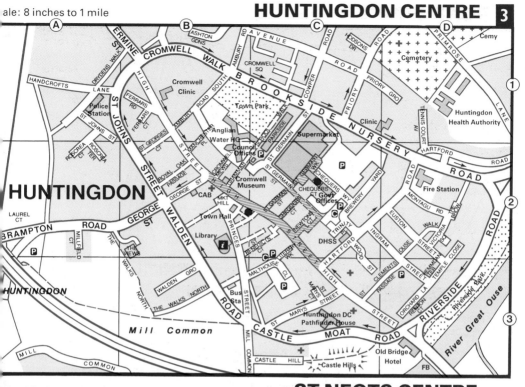

Scale: 8 inches to 1 mile

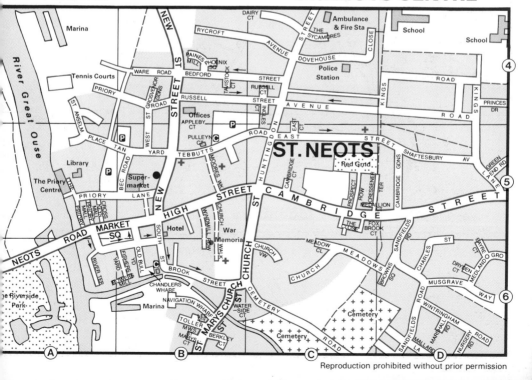

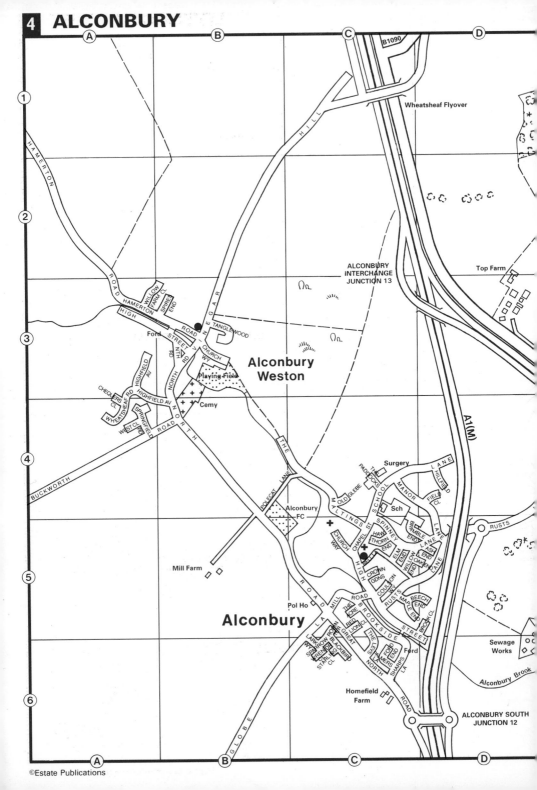

Alconbury
Weston

Alconbury

B1090
Wheatsheaf Flyover

ALCONBURY
INTERCHANGE
JUNCTION 13

Top Farm

A1(M)

RUSTS

Surgery

Sch

Sewage
Works

Alconbury Brook

ALCONBURY SOUTH
JUNCTION 12

HAMERTON ROAD

WILLOW FARM CL
SPIRES END
HIGH HAMERTON
Ford
STREET
NTH RD
ROAD
NENGAR
CHURCH WY
Tanglewood
Playing Field
Cemy
CHEQUERS CL
WHEATSHEAF RD
WEST CL
HIGHFIELD AV
HIGHFIELD AV
SPRINGFIELD
ROAD
NORTH
BUCKWORTH

THE LANE

POLECAT LANE

Alconbury
FC

Mill Farm

Pol Ho

MILL ROAD

MALTINGS
OLD GLEBE
THE PADDOCKS
SCHOOL LANE
MANOR
HILLFIELD CL
SPINNEY
CHAPEL ST
CHURCH WAY
HAW THORN END
ELM END
OAKS END
WILLOW END
ASH END
CROWN GDNS
COULTON RUSTS
MAPLE END
BEECH END
BRAMBLE END
HIGH STREET
BROOK CL

LARKSPUR
SPARROW ROAD
WRENS
STARLING CL
BLACKBIRD
GREAT NORTH ROAD
THE MERE
THE RED
BROOKSIDE
THE LEYS
PALMERS
SHARPS LA
Ford

Homefield
Farm

GLOBE ROAD

©Estate Publications

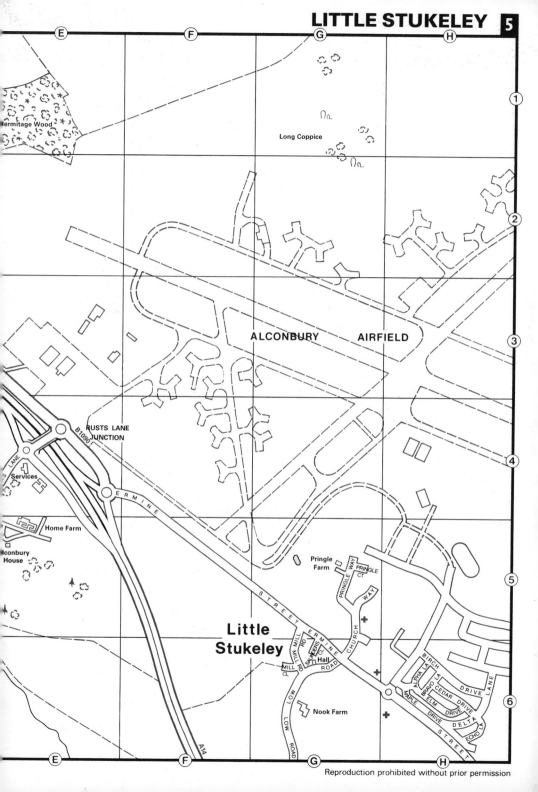

E   F   G   H

1

ermitage Wood

Long Coppice

2

3

ALCONBURY   AIRFIELD

RUSTS LANE
JUNCTION
B1090

4

's LANE

Services

ERMINE

Home Farm

lconbury
House

Pringle
Farm

PRINGLE WAY
PRINGLE
CT

5

WAY

Little
Stukeley

STREET ERMINE

CHURCH ROAD

BIRCH

ALPHA LA

CEDAR DRIVE

BRAVO

ELM DRIVE

MILL RD
MILL RD
SAWYERS CL
Hall
MILL
CL

MAPLE

DELTA

DRIVE

LANE

ECHO LA

Nook Farm

STREET

LOW ROAD

A14

E   F   G   H

6

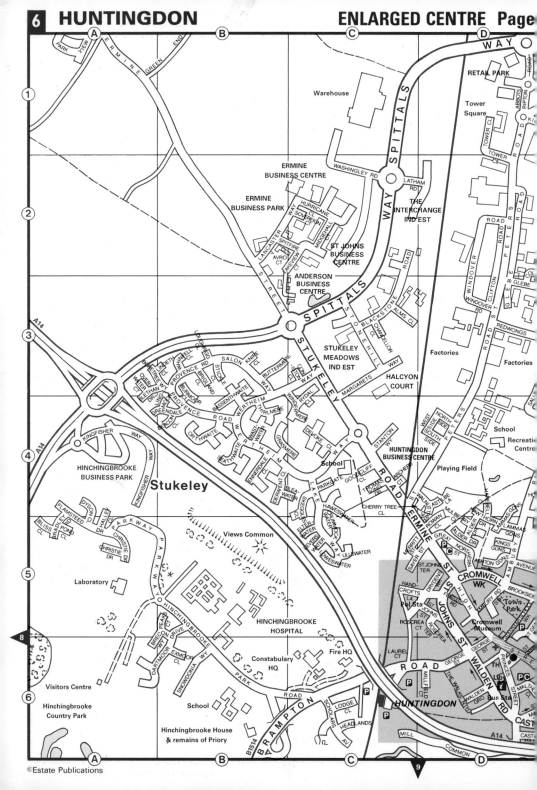

©Estate Publications

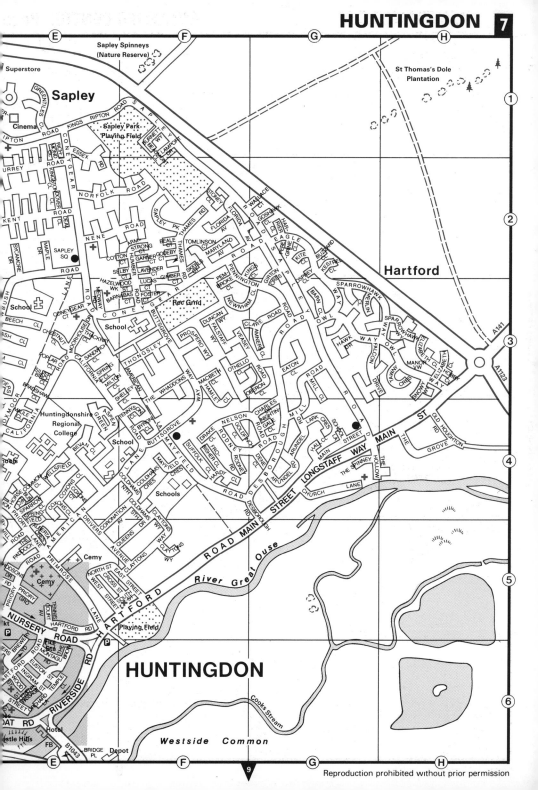

Sapley Spinneys
(Nature Reserve)

Superstore

St Thomas's Dole
Plantation

Sapley

Cinema

Sapley Park
Playing Field

Hartford

Rec Grnd

School

School

School

Huntingdonshire
Regional
College

School

Schools

Cemy

Cemy

NURSERY ROAD

Playing Field

HUNTINGDON

River Great Ouse

Cooks Stream

Hotel

Depot

Westside Common

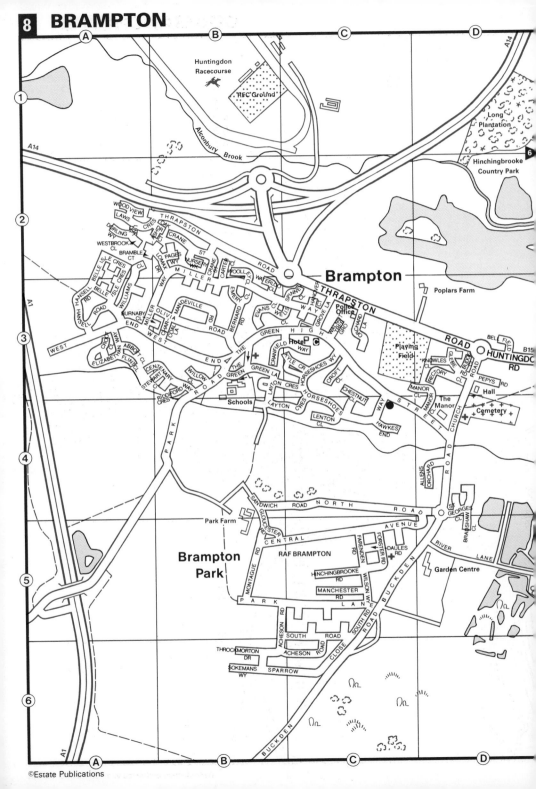

8 BRAMPTON

Huntingdon Racecourse

RFC Ground

Alconbury Brook

A14

A14

Long Plantation

Hinchingbrooke Country Park

Brampton

Poplars Farm

THRAPSTON ROAD

WOOD VIEW
LAWS
DARLING WY
OAK DR
CRES
CRANE ST
CARTER
WOOLLEY CL
WAY
ERLOW
SPINNEY
HANSER
GROVE LA
WARD LA
ORCHARD LA
Police Office

THRAPSTON

WESTBROOK CL
BRAMBLE CT
PAGES WY
NURSERY
LOMAX
MILLER WAY
EMERY RD
EVANS CL
H G
HJG
THE GREEN
CRANFIELD RD
Hotel C
GREEN WAY
LAYTON CRES
HORSESHOES WY
CROFT CL
CHESTNUT
WAY
Playing Field

BELLE ISLE CRES
BELLE ISLE CRES
HANSELL RD
WILLIAMS
BURNABY CLT
MILLER END
OLIVIA CHAP LA
MANDEVILLE RD
BERNARD RD
COAL LA
GREEN LA
PYLE CR
HORSESHOES CRES
LENTON CL
HAWKES END
MANOR
The Manor
Hall
KNOWLES
GLEBE RD
RECTORY
PEPYS RD
Cemetery

HANSELL ROAD
WEST
CROFT WY
ABBOTT CL
FLINTCL
ELIZABETH
CENTENARY WY
WILLOW WAY
STEWART
RIDDLES CRES
CRANFORD WAY
LAYTON
Schools
LAYTON
THE GREEN

WEST END
WEST END ROAD

PARK ROAD

STREET
CHURCH
ROAD

HUNTINGDON RD
BEL FIELD
B15
ROAD
BUCKDEN RD

ALLENS ORCHARD

SANDWICH ROAD
NORTH
ROAD
St GEORGES
BRADSHAW CL
RIVER LANE

Park Farm

Brampton Park

MONTAGUE RD
GLOUCESTER RD
CENTRAL
AVENUE
RAF BRAMPTON
FARENDEN RD
FORSTER RD
DAULES RD
HINCHINGBROOKE RD
MANCHESTER RD
WILSON WY
BUCKDEN RD

PARK LANE
Garden Centre

ACHESON RD
SOUTH ROAD
ACHESON ROAD
THROCKMORTON DR
SOKEMANS WY
SPARROW
CLOSE
SOUTH ROAD

BUCKDEN

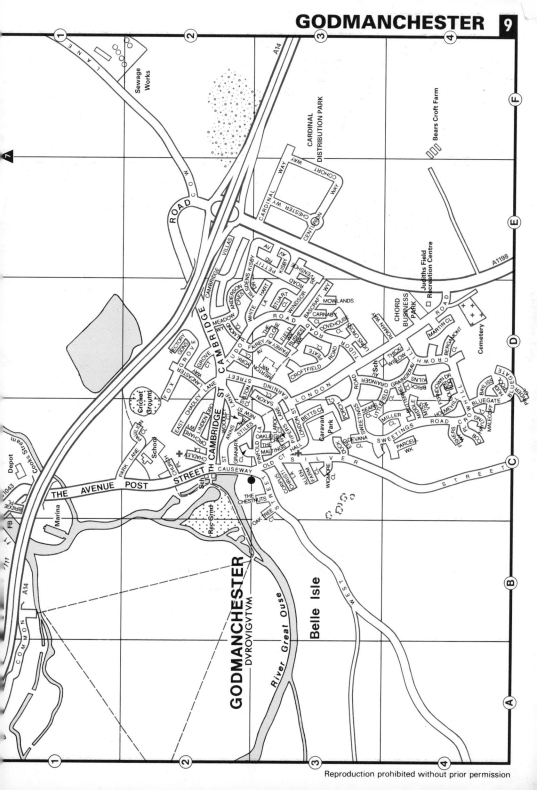

GODMANCHESTER
DVROVIGVTVM

Belle Isle

River Great Ouse

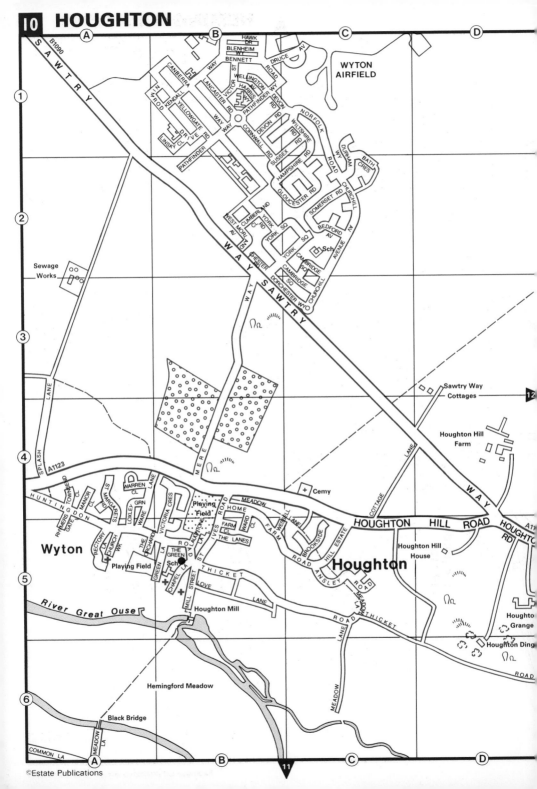

A B C D

1

WYTON AIRFIELD

HAWK CL
BLENHEIM WY
BENNETT
DRUCE AV
WELLINGTON AV
VICTOR ST
HARRIS RD
PATHFINDER RD
DEVON WY
NORFOLK RD
WILTSHIRE RD
WAY
LANCASTER RD
CORNWALL RD
DEVON RD
SUSSEX RD
HAMPSHIRE RD
GLOUCESTER RD
SOMERSET RD
DURHAM WY
BATH CRES
CHURCHILL RD
CANBERRA
KENDALL RD
YELLOWGATE
DRIVE
LINSAY CL
PATHFINDER RD

2

Sewage Works

WEST MORL AV
CUMBERLAND CL
YORK RD
CHESTER WY
DORCHESTER WY
SAWTRY WAY
YORK SQ
YORK SQ
CAMBRIDGE SQ
CAMBRIDGE SQ
CHURCHILL SQ
BEDFORD AV
YORK SO
AVENUE
Sch

3

Sawtry Way Cottages

12

Houghton Hill Farm

4

SPLASH LANE
A1123
MERE LANE
HUNTINGDON RD
RHYNER TOWNSEND GATE CL
ST MARGARETS CL
MANOR CL
WARREN CL
THE WARE
LOXLEY GRN
VICTORIA CRES
LAKESIDE
MEADOW ROAD
HOME FARM CL
IVES WARD CL
RUSSELL LANE
BROOKSIDE
HILL ESTATE
COTTAGE LANE
Cemy
Playing Field
HOUGHTON HILL ROAD
HOUGHTON RD
A11
WAY

5

Wyton
RECTORY LA
CHURCH WK
THE ORCHARD
GREEN LA
THE GREEN
Sch
CHAPEL
LACKSTONE
ST IVES
THE LANES
FARM RD
ANSLEY ROAD
Houghton Hill House
Houghton Grange
Playing Field
THICKET
MILL STREET
LOVE LANE
MEADOW LANE
Houghton Ding
ROAD

River Great Ouse
Houghton Mill
Houghton

6

Hemingford Meadow

Black Bridge

COMMON LA
MEADOW LA

A B C D

11

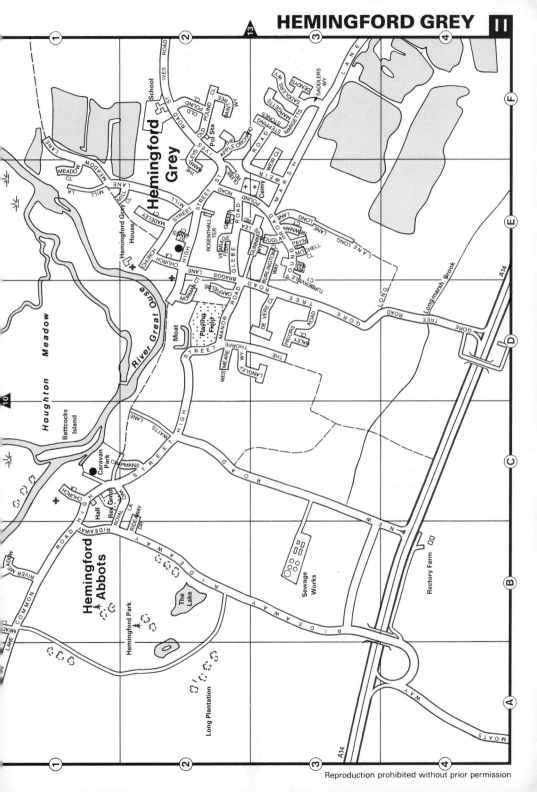

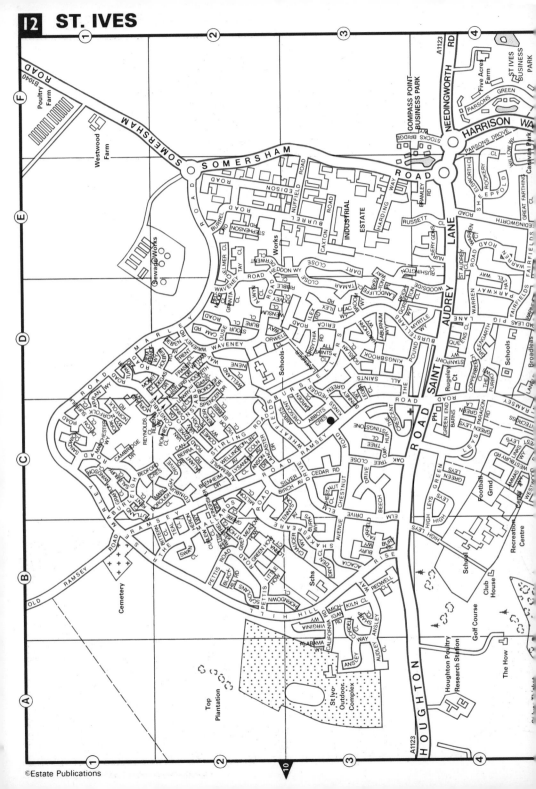

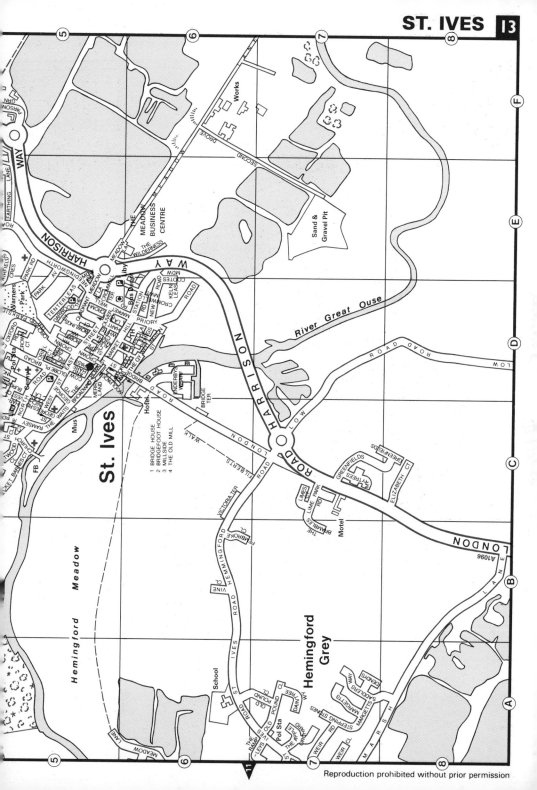

St. Ives

Hemingford Grey

Hemingford Meadow

River Great Ouse

1 BRIDGE HOUSE
2 BRIDGEFOOT HOUSE
3 MILLSIDE
4 THE OLD MILL

Works

Sand & Gravel Pit

THE MEADOW BUSINESS CENTRE

THE WILDERNESS

School

Pol Sta

Motel

Greenfields

HARRISON WAY

LONDON ROAD

LOW ROAD

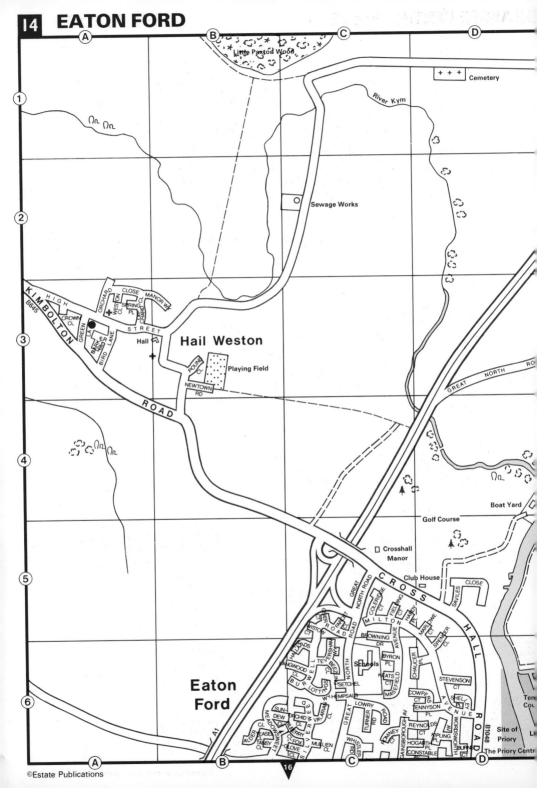

A B C D

1

2

3

4

5

6

Little Paxton Wood

River Kym

+ + + Cemetery

Sewage Works

KIMBOLTON
B645
HIGH
CROWN
CL
GREEN LA
BARKER CL
BIRD LANE
ORCHARD CL
WESTON CL
CLOSE
SPRING PL
MANOR WY
CHARD
STREET
Hall
Hail Weston
POUND CL
NEWTOWN RD
ROAD
Playing Field

GREAT NORTH RD

Boat Yard

Golf Course

□ Crosshall Manor

Club House
CROSS HALL
CLOSE
SAVILES

GREAT NORTH ROAD
COLERIDGE
FIELDING
HARDY
MARLOWE
SPENCER CL
MILTON
BROWNING DR
AVENUE
BYRON PL
CHAUCER PL
STEVENSON CT
SHELLEY CL
Schools
KEATS CT
MASEFIELD
COWPER CT
TENNYSON PL
AVENUE ROAD
MARVELL RD
LANGWOOD
BURWELL
LOTTINGS
TEVERSHAM
HEMPSALS
VARIAN W
SETCHEL
HALLARDS
WISTON CT
GREAT NORTH ROAD
LOWRY RD
ROMNEY RD
GAINSBROUGH AV
REYNOLDS
SUN-DEW
ORCHID
ALDER CL
TEASEL
PANSY CL
GLOVE CL
FOX CL
MULLIEN CL
SILVERWEED
MEADOWSWEET CL
BERRY CL
TURNER RD
HOGARTH PL
CONSTABLE AV
KIPLING
THOMSBROW
BURNS
WHISTLER
CL
A1

Eaton Ford

B1048

Site of Priory
The Priory Centre

Ten
Cou
Li

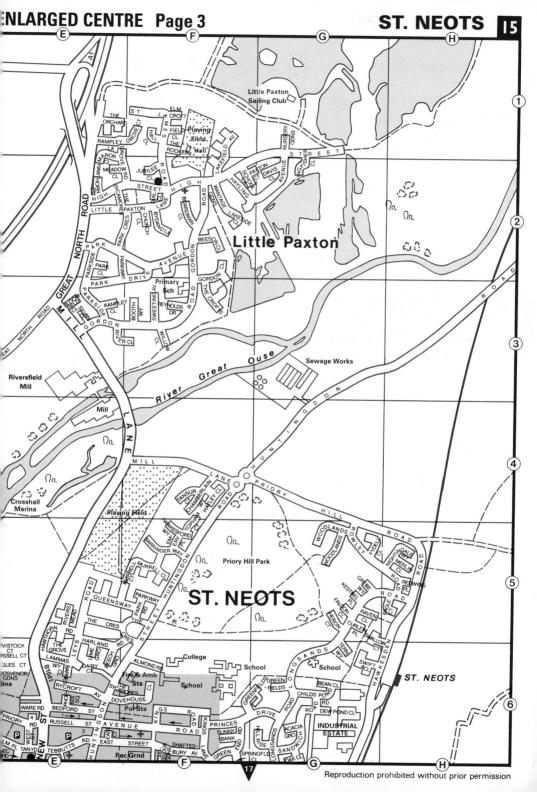

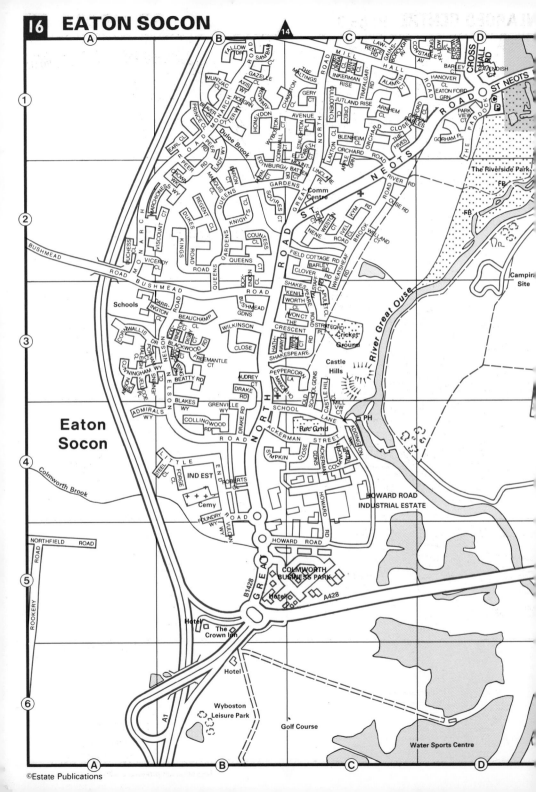

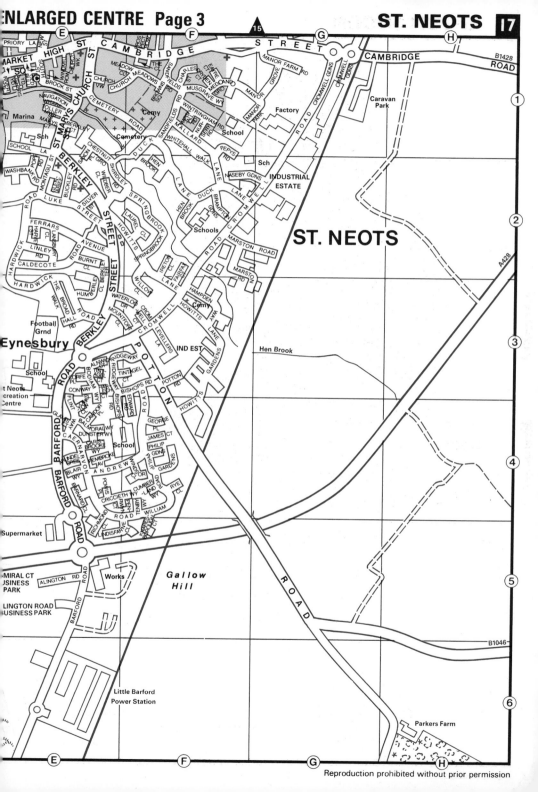

ST. NEOTS

Eynesbury

Gallow Hill

Little Barford Power Station

Parkers Farm

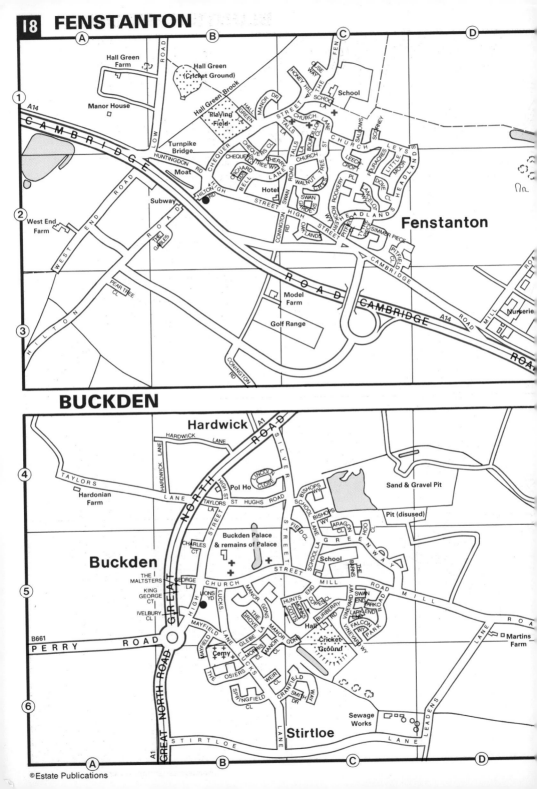

18 FENSTANTON

BUCKDEN

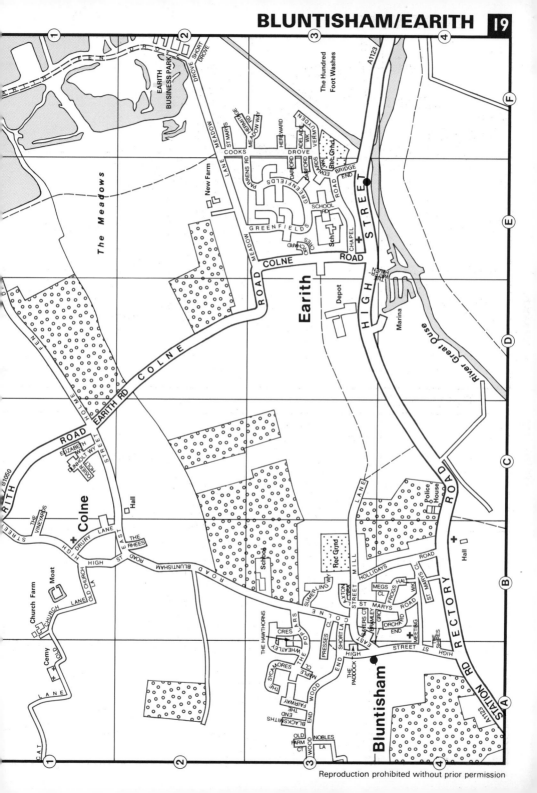

A - Z INDEX TO STREETS
with Postcodes

The Index includes some names for which there is insufficient space on the maps. These names are preceded by an * and are followed by the nearest adjoining thoroughfare.

HUNTINGDON

Abbbots Ripton Rd. PE28   6 D1
Abbots Cres. PE27   12 C3
Abbott Clo. PE28   8 A3
Acacia Av. PE27   12 B3
Acheson Rd. PE28   8 B6
Adelaide Wk. PE27   19 F3
Alabama Way. PE27   12 A3
Albemarle Rd. PE27   12 C2
Alberta Cres. PE29   7 E5
Alder Clo. PE29   6 D5
Alexandra Ct. PE27   13 D5
All Saints Clo. PE27   12 D3
All Saints Grn. PE27   12 D3
Allen Farm Clo. PE29   9 C3
Allens Orchard. PE28   8 D4
Almond Clo. PE29   9 D2
Alms Clo. PE29   6 C3
Alpha La. PE28   5 H6
Alwyn Clo. PE27   12 D2
Ambury Hill. PE29   6 D5
Ambury Rd. PE29   3 B1
Ambury Rd Sth. PE29   3 B1
American La. PE27   7 E5
Amners Clo. PE29   7 G3
Anderson Cres. PE29   9 D2
Ansley Rd. PE28   10 C5
Ansley Way. PE27   12 A3
Anson Dri. PE27   12 C2
Aragon Clo. PE19   18 C5
Archers Ct. PE29   6 C4
Armstrong Ct. PE29   7 F2
Arran Way. PE27   12 C1
Arundel Rd. PE29   7 G4
Ash Clo. PE29   7 E3
Ash Ct. PE29   8 B2
Ash End. PE28   4 D5
Aspen Grn. PE29   7 E4
Astilbe La. PE29   6 D4
Audley Clo. PE27   12 A3
Avenue Rd. PE29   3 C1
Avro Ct. PE29   6 B2

Barn Clo. PE29   7 G3
Barnes Ct. PE27   13 C5
*Barringer Ct,
  London St. PE29   9 C3
Bascraft Way. PE29   9 D3
Bassenthwaite. PE29   6 B4
Bath Cres. PE28   10 C2
Bayliss. PE29   9 D4
Beacon Clo. PE29   6 B4
Beale Ct. PE29   7 F2
Beaumont Clo. PE29   7 F1
Bedford Av. PE28   10 C2
Bedford Cres. PE27   12 C1
Beech Clo. PE29   7 E3
Beech Dri. PE27   12 C3
Beech End. PE28   4 C5
Bell Field. PE28   8 D3
Bell La, Alconbury. PE28   4 C5
Bell La,
  Fenstanton. PE28   18 B2
Belle Isle Cres. PE28   8 A2
Bennett Rd. PE28   10 B1
Bergamont Clo. PE29   9 D4
Bernard Clo. PE27   7 E4
Bernard Rd. PE28   8 B3
Betts Clo. PE29   9 C3
Bevan Clo. PE29   7 E4
Birch Dri. PE28   5 H6
*Birt La,
  Wellington St. PE27   13 D6
Bishops Way. PE19   18 C4
Bittern Clo. PE27   12 B2
Black Hill Rd. PE27   12 B2
Blackbird Way. PE28   9 D4
Blacksmiths End. PE28   19 A3
Blackstone Rd. PE29   6 C3

Bleawater. PE29   6 C4
Blenheim Dri. PE27   12 C2
Blenheim Way. PE28   10 B1
Blethan Dri. PE29   6 A3
Bliss Clo. PE29   6 A5
Bluntisham Rd. PE28   19 B2
Boretree Way. PE29   6 A3
Bourdillon Clo. PE28   18 C1
Bowlings Ct. PE27   13 D5
Bradley Rd. PE29   6 A5
Bradshaw Clo,
  Brampton. PE28   8 D5
Bradshaw Clo,
  Huntingdon. PE29   7 E3
Braggs La. PE28   11 E2
Bramble Clo. PE29   8 A2
Bramble Ct. PE28   4 C5
Bramble End. PE28   4 C5
Bramley Gro. PE28   19 B3
Bramley Rd. PE27   12 E4
Brampton Rd. PE29   3 A2
Bravo La. PE28   5 H6
Brecon Way. PE29   6 B6
Brewery Yd. PE29   3 C2
Brick Kilns. PE29   9 D4
Bridge End. PE28   19 E3
Bridge House. PE27   13 D6
Bridge St. PE27   13 D6
Bridge Ter. PE27   13 C6
*Bridge View,
  Wellington St. PE27   13 D6
Bridgefoot House. PE27   13 D6
Brigland Clo. PE29   6 B3
Broad Leas. PE27   12 D4
*Broad Leas Ct,
  Oxford St. PE27   13 D5
Brook Clo. PE28   4 D5
Brookside,
  Alconbury. PE28   4 C5
Brookside,
  Houghton. PE28   10 C5
Brookside,
  Huntingdon. PE29   3 B1
Broom Way. PE27   12 D3
Buckden Rd. PE28   8 B6
Buckworth Rd. PE28   4 A4
Budge Clo. PE28   8 D3
Bull La. PE27   13 D6
Burberry Rd. PE19   18 C5
Bure Clo. PE27   12 D2
Burgess Wk. PE27   13 D5
Burleigh Rd. PE27   12 C1
*Burleigh Ter,
  St Johns Rd. PE27   13 D5
Burlington Way. PE28   11 E3
Burmoor Clo. PE29   6 B4
Burnaby Clo. PE28   8 A3
Burnett Way. PE29   7 F1
Burns Way. PE27   12 B3
Burrel Rd. PE27   12 E2
Bursellars. PE27   12 D3
Bury Clo. PE27   12 B3
Bury Way. PE27   12 B3
Bushey Clo. PE29   7 E4
Buttermel Clo. PE29   9 D4
Buttermere. PE29   6 B3
Buttersgrove Way. PE29   7 F3
Buzzard Clo. PE29   7 G2
Byron Clo. PE29   7 F4

California Rd,
  Huntingdon. PE29   7 E3
California Rd,
  St Ives. PE27   12 B3
Cam Rd. PE27   12 D2
Cambridge Dri. PE27   12 C1
Cambridge Rd,
  Fenstanton. PE28   18 A1
Cambridge Rd,
  Godmanchester. PE29   9 D2
Cambridge St. PE28   10 C2
Cambridge St. PE29   9 C2
Cambridge Villas. PE29   9 D2
Canberra Dri. PE27   12 C2
Canberra Way. PE28   10 B1
Cardinal Way. PE29   9 E3
Carnaby Clo. PE29   9 D3
Carter St. PE28   8 B2
Castle Hill. PE28   3 C3
*Castle Hill Ct,
  High St. PE29   3 C3

Castle Moat Rd. PE29   3 C3
Cat La. PE28   19 A1
Causeway. PE29   9 C2
Caxton Rd. PE27   12 E3
Cedar Dri. PE28   5 H6
Cedar Rd. PE27   12 C3
Centenary Way. PE28   8 B3
Central Av. PE28   8 B5
Centurion Way. PE29   9 E3
Chadley La. PE29   9 C2
Chancellor Clo. PE29   6 C3
*Chapel Ct,
  Chapel La. PE27   13 D6
Chapel La,
  Houghton. PE28   10 B5
Chapel La,
  St Ives. PE27   13 D6
Chapel Rd. PE28   19 E3
Chapel St. PE28   4 C5
Chapmans. PE28   11 C2
Charcoal La. PE28   8 B3
Charles Ct. PE19   18 B5
Charles Dri. PE29   7 G4
Chaucer Way. PE27   12 B3
Chelmer Way. PE27   12 E2
Chequer St. PE28   18 B2
Chequers Clo,
  Alconbury Weston.
  PE28   4 A3
Chequers Clo,
  Fenstanton. PE28   18 B1
Chequers Ct,
  Fenstanton. PE28   18 B2
Chequers Clo,
  Huntingdon. PE29   3 C2
Chequers Way. PE29   3 C2
Cherry Tree Clo. PE29   6 D4
Cherry Tree Way. PE28   18 B2
Chester Rd. PE28   10 B2
Chester Way. PE29   9 E3
Chestnut Clo,
  Brampton. PE28   8 C4
Chestnut Clo,
  Huntingdon. PE28   7 E3
Chestnut Clo,
  St Ives. PE27   12 C3
Chestnut Rd. PE27   12 C3
Christie Dri. PE29   6 A5
Church La,
  Fenstanton. PE28   18 C1
Church La,
  Hartford. PE29   7 G4
Church La,
  Hemingford Abbots.
  PE28   11 C1
Church La,
  Hemingford Grey.
  PE28   11 E2
Church Leys. PE28   18 C1
Church Pl. PE29   9 C2
Church Rd. PE28   8 D4
Church St,
  Buckden. PE19   18 B5
Church St,
  Fenstanton. PE28   18 C2
Church St,
  Hemingford Grey.
  PE28   11 E2
Church St, St Ives. PE27   13 C5
Church Walk. PE28   10 A5
Church Way,
  Alconbury. PE28   4 C5
Church Way,
  Alconbury Weston.
  PE28   4 B3
Church Way,
  Little Stukeley. PE28   5 G6
Churchill Av. PE28   10 C2
*Churchill Hall, St Ives
  Business Pk. PE27   12 F4
Clare Ct. PE27   13 C5
*Clare Hall, St Ives
  Business Pk. PE27   12 F4
Clare Rd. PE29   7 G3
Claytons Way. PE29   7 F5
Clifton Rd. PE29   6 D3
Cob Pl. PE28   8 B5
Cohort Way. PE29   9 E3
Coldhams Cres. PE29   7 F4
Coldhams Nth. PE29   7 F4

Coldhams Sth. PE29   7 F4
Colne Rd,
  Bluntisham. PE28   19 B3
Colne Rd, Earith. PE28   19 D2
Colour Clo. PE29   6 D3
Comet Way. PE27   12 C2
Common La. PE28   11 A1
Coneygear Ct. PE29   7 E3
Coneygear Rd. PE29   7 E1
Conington Rd. PE28   18 B2
Coniston Clo. PE29   6 B3
Constable Rd. PE27   12 C2
Cooks Drove. PE28   19 F2
Cootes Mdw. PE27   13 D6
Copes Clo. PE19   18 C5
Copperbeech Clo. PE27   12 D4
Cordell Clo. PE27   12 B3
Cornwall Rd. PE28   10 B1
Coronation Av. PE27   7 E5
Corpus Christi La. PE29   9 C3
Cottage La. PE28   10 C4
Cotton Ct. PE29   7 F2
Coulson Way. PE28   4 C5
Cow and Hare Passage.
  PE27   13 D5
Cow La. PE29   9 E2
Cowper Rd. PE27   3 C1
Coxons Clo. PE29   7 E4
Coxons Ct. PE29   7 E4
Crane St. PE28   8 B2
Cranfield Way,
  Brampton. PE28   8 B3
Cranfield Way,
  Buckden. PE19   18 B6
Croft Clo. PE28   8 C3
Croftfield Rd. PE29   9 D3
Cromwell Mews,
  Huntingdon. PE29   3 B2
Cromwell Mews,
  St Ives. PE27   13 D6
Cromwell Pl. PE27   13 D5
Cromwell Sq. PE29   3 C1
Cromwell Ter. PE27   13 D5
Cromwell Wk. PE27   3 B1
Croot Clo. PE28   8 A3
Cross St. PE29   9 C4
Crowhill. PE29   9 C4
*Crown Clo,
  Broad Leas. PE27   13 D5
Crown Ct. PE27   13 D5
Crown Gdns. PE29   4 C5
Crown Pl. PE27   13 D5
Crown St. PE27   13 D5
*Crown St Mews,
  Crown St. PE27   13 D5
Crown Wk. PE27   13 D5
Crummock Water. PE29   6 C5
Cumberland Clo. PE28   10 B2
Curlew Clo. PE27   12 B2

Da Vinci Clo. PE27   12 C2
Daintree Way. PE28   11 F2
*Dallington Ct,
  Trinity Pl. PE27   3 C2
Darford. PE28   19 E3
Dart Clo. PE27   12 E3
Dartmoor Dri. PE28   6 B6
Darwood Ct. PE27   13 D5
Daules Rd. PE28   8 C5
De Vere Clo. PE28   11 D3
Deal Clo. PE29   7 E2
Deben Av. PE27   12 D2
Degas Clo. PE27   12 D2
Deighton Clo. PE29   7 F4
Delta Dri. PE28   5 H6
Dendys. PE28   11 F3
Dene Clo. PE29   7 G4
Derwent Clo,
  St Ives. PE27   12 E2
Derwent Clo,
  Stukeley. PE29   6 B4
Desborough Rd. PE29   7 G4
Devana Clo. PE29   9 C3
Devoke Clo. PE29   6 C4
Devon Clo. PE27   12 C1
Devon Rd. PE28   10 B1
Dorchester Way. PE28   10 B3
Dorling Way. PE28   8 A2
Douglas Clo. PE28   11 E3
Dove Clo. PE29   18 C2

Dovehouse Clo. PE29   9 D3
Dover Clo. PE28   7 E2
Dovey Clo. PE27   12 D2
*Downing Hall, St Ives
  Business Pk. PE27   12 F4
Drake Clo. PE29   7 F4
Drivers Av. PE29   7 E5
Druce Av. PE28   10 B1
Drury La. PE28   19 B1
Dryden Clo. PE27   12 B3
Drydens Wk. PE29   3 A1
Duck End. PE29   9 C3
*Duncan Ho, High St,
  Earith. PE28   19 E3
Duncan Way. PE29   7 F3
Dunholt Way. PE28   19 C1
Durham Way. PE28   10 C2
Dyson Clo. PE29   6 A4

Eagle Way. PE28   7 G2
Earith Fen Drove. PE28   19 F1
Earith Rd. PE28   19 C1
Earning St. PE29   9 D3
East Chadley La. PE29   9 D2
East St,
  Bluntisham. PE28   19 A3
East St, Colne. PE28   19 B2
East St,
  Huntingdon. PE29   7 F5
East St, St Ives. PE27   13 D5
Eaton Clo. PE29   7 G3
Echo La. PE28   5 H6
Edinburgh Dri. PE27   12 C2
Edison Rd. PE27   12 E3
Edwards Wk. PE28   19 E3
Elizabeth Clo. PE29   7 H3
Elizabeth Ct. PE27   13 C7
Elizabeth Way. PE28   19 C1
Elizabethan Way. PE28   8 A3
Elm Clo. PE29   7 E3
Elm Dri,
  Little Stukeley. PE28   5 H6
Elm Dri, St Ives. PE27   12 C3
Elm End. PE28   4 C5
Elsworth Clo. PE27   12 E4
Elterwater. PE29   6 C6
Emery Clo. PE28   8 B3
*Emmanuel Hall, St Ives
  Business Pk. PE27   12 F4
Enderbys Wharf. PE27   13 D6
Ennerdale Clo. PE29   6 B4
Erica Rd. PE27   12 D3
*Ermine Ct,
  Ermine St. PE29   6 D4
Ermine St,
  Gt Stukeley. PE28   6 A1
Ermine St,
  Huntingdon. PE29   3 B1
Ermine St,
  Little Stukeley. PE28   5 G1
Essex Rd. PE29   7 E1
Euston St. PE29   3 D1
Evans Clo. PE28   8 B1
Exmoor Clo. PE29   6 B6

Fairey Av. PE29   9 D1
Fairfield. PE27   12 B1
Fairfields. PE27   12 D1
Fairfields Cres. PE28   13 E1
Falcon Dri. PE29   7 G2
Falcon Way,
  Buckden. PE19   18 C5
Falcon Way,
  Hartford. PE29   7 G1
Falstaff Way. PE29   7 F1
Farenden Rd. PE28   8 C1
Farm Clo. PE28   10 B1
Farthing La. PE27   13 E1
Ferndown Dri. PE29   9 D1
Ferrars Ct. PE29   3 B1
Ferrars Rd. PE29   3 B1
Field Clo,
  Alconbury. PE28   4 D1
Field Clo,
  Buckden. PE19   18 C5
Field Wk. PE29   9 D1
Filberts Wk. PE27   13 C1
Fishers Way. PE29   9 C1
Flamsteed Dri. PE29   6 A1
Flint Clo. PE28   8 A1

Florida Av. PE29 — 7 F2
Ford End. PE28 — 4 C6
Forster Rd. PE28 — 8 C5
Forsythia Rd. PE27 — 12 D3
Foster Ct. PE29 — 7 F3
*Foundry Wk,
  Market Hill. PE27 — 13 D5
Four Acres. PE28 — 18 C2
Fox Gro. PE29 — 9 D2
Fraser Dri. PE27 — 12 D2
*Free Church Pass,
  Market Hill. PE27 — 13 D5
Frobisher Clo. PE29 — 7 F4
Frogs Hall. PE28 — 19 B4

Gainsborough Dri.
  PE27 — 12 D2
Garden Clo. PE27 — 12 D3
Garner Ct. PE29 — 7 F2
George La. PE19 — 18 B5
George St. PE29 — 3 B2
George Yd. PE27 — 13 C5
Gimber Ct. PE29 — 7 F2
Girton Cres. PE29 — 7 G2
Glebe La. PE19 — 18 B5
Glebe Rd,
  Brampton. PE28 — 8 D3
Glebe Rd,
  Hemingford Grey.
  PE28 — 11 E2
Glebe Rd,
  Huntingdon. PE29 — 6 D3
Globe La. PE28 — 4 B6
Gloucester Rd,
  Brampton. PE28 — 8 B4
Gloucester Rd,
  Wyton. PE28 — 10 B2
Godeby Ct. PE29 — 7 F2
Golden Rod. PE29 — 9 D4
Goldfinch Clo. PE29 — 7 F4
Goodcliff Clo. PE29 — 6 C4
Gore Tree Rd. PE28 — 11 D3
Gorse Way. PE27 — 12 D3
Goshawk Clo. PE27 — 7 G2
Gosslan Clo. PE27 — 12 D3
Grafton Clo. PE27 — 12 C1
Grainger Av. PE29 — 9 D3
Grammar School Wk.
  PE29 — 3 B2
Granary Clo. PE29 — 9 C2
Granta Clo. PE27 — 12 D2
Grasmere. PE29 — 6 B4
Great Farthing Clo.
  PE27 — 12 E4
Great How. PE27 — 12 B2
Great North Rd,
  Alconbury. PE28 — 4 C5
Great North Rd,
  Buckden. PE19 — 18 B5
Great Northern St. PE29 — 6 D5
Grebe Clo. PE27 — 12 C2
Green Clo. PE28 — 11 E2
Green End Barns. PE27 — 12 C4
Green End. PE28 — 6 A1
Green How. PE27 — 12 B2
Green La,
  Brampton. PE28 — 8 B3
Green La,
  St Ives. PE27 — 12 C4
Green La,
  Wyton. PE28 — 10 B5
Green Leys. PE27 — 12 C4
Greendale. PE29 — 6 B4
Greenfields,
  Earith. PE28 — 19 E3
Greenfields,
  St Ives. PE27 — 13 C7
Greengarth. PE27 — 12 D4
Greentiles Clo. PE27 — 7 E1
Greenway. PE19 — 18 C5
Grove Ct,
  Godmanchester. PE29 — 9 D2
Grove Ct,
  Broad Leas
  St Ives. PE27 — 13 D5
Grove La. PE28 — 8 C3
Gunnings Way. PE28 — 11 E3
aley Clo. PE28 — 11 D3
all Clo. PE29 — 7 G4
all Green La. PE28 — 18 B1
alley Way. PE28 — 6 A5
amerton Rd. PE28 — 4 A3
amlet Clo. PE29 — 7 F3
ampshire Rd. PE28 — 10 C2
andcrofts La. PE29 — 3 A1

Hanover Ct. PE28 — 8 C3
Hansell Rd. PE28 — 8 A3
Harding Way. PE27 — 12 E3
Harebell Clo. PE29 — 6 D4
Hardwick La. PE19 — 18 B4
Hardy Clo. PE29 — 7 F4
Harrier Clo. PE29 — 7 G2
Harris Way. PE28 — 10 B1
Harrison Way. PE27 — 12 F4
Hartford Rd. PE29 — 3 C3
Harvest Ct. PE27 — 13 C5
Haweswater. PE18 — 6 C4
Hawk Dri,
  Hartford. PE29 — 7 G3
Hawk Dri, Wyton. PE28 — 10 B1
Hawkes End. PE28 — 8 C4
Hawthorn Dri. PE29 — 6 D4
Hawthorn End. PE28 — 4 C5
Hawthorn Way. PE27 — 12 D3
Hayling Clo. PE29 — 9 C4
Hazel Way. PE27 — 12 D4
Hazelwood Wk. PE27 — 7 F3
Headlands,
  Fenstanton. PE28 — 18 C2
Headlands,
  Huntingdon. PE29 — 6 C6
Heddon Way. PE27 — 12 E2
Hemingford Rd. PE27 — 13 B6
Hemmdan Ter. PE29 — 3 D3
Hereward. PE28 — 19 F3
Hermitage Rd. PE28 — 19 F2
Heron Way. PE27 — 12 B2
High Leys. PE27 — 12 B4
High St,
  Alconbury. PE28 — 4 C5
High St, Alconbury
  Weston. PE28 — 4 A3
High St,
  Bluntisham. PE28 — 19 A3
High St,
  Brampton. PE28 — 8 A3
High St, Buckden. PE19 — 18 B5
High St, Colne. PE28 — 19 B1
High St, Earith. PE28 — 19 D3
High St,
  Fenstanton. PE28 — 18 B2
High St,
  Hemingford Abbots.
  PE28 — 11 C1
High St, Hemingford
  Grey. PE28 — 11 E2
High St,
  Huntingdon. PE29 — 3 B1
Highfield Av. PE28 — 4 A3
Hill Estate. PE28 — 10 C5
Hill Rise. PE27 — 12 B2
Hillfield. PE28 — 4 D4
Hilsdens Dri. PE28 — 9 D2
Hilton Rd. PE28 — 18 A3
Hinchingbrooke Pk Rd.
  PE29 — 6 B5
Hinchingbrooke Rd.
  PE28 — 8 C5
Hobby Clo. PE29 — 7 H3
Hodsons Dri. PE29 — 3 C1
Hogarth Clo. PE27 — 12 D2
Holbein Rd. PE27 — 12 D2
Hollidays Rd. PE28 — 19 B3
Holme Fen Drove. PE28 — 19 C1
Holmehill. PE28 — 9 C4
Home Farm Rd. PE28 — 10 B4
Honey Hill. PE28 — 18 C1
Hoo Clo. PE19 — 18 C5
Horse Common Clo.
  PE29 — 7 E4
Horse Common La.
  PE29 — 6 D4
Horseshoes Way. PE28 — 8 C3
Houghton Hill Rd. PE28 — 10 C5
Houghton Rd. PE27 — 12 A4
Hudpool. PE29 — 9 D4
Humber Rd. PE29 — 7 F2
Huntingdon Rd,
  Brampton. PE28 — 8 D3
Huntingdon Rd,
  Fenstanton. PE28 — 18 B2
Huntingdon Rd,
  Houghton. PE28 — 10 A4
Hunts End. PE19 — 18 C5
Hurricane Clo. PE29 — 6 C2
Hurstingstone. PE27 — 12 C3

Ilex End. PE28 — 12 D3

INDUSTRIAL & RETAIL:
Anderson Business Centre.
  PE29 — 6 C3
Cardinal Distribution Pk.
  PE29 — 9 F3
Chord Business Pk.
  PE29 — 9 D4
Compass Point
  Business Pk. PE27 — 12 F4
Earith Business Pk.
  PE28 — 19 F2
Ermine Business
  Centre. PE29 — 6 C2
Ermine Business Pk.
  PE29 — 6 B2
Halcyon Ct. PE29 — 6 C3
Hinchingbrooke
  Business Pk. PE29 — 6 A4
Huntingdon Business
  Centre. PE29 — 6 C4
St Ives Business Pk.
St Johns Business Centre.
  PE29 — 6 C2
Stukeley Meadows
  Ind Est. PE29 — 6 C3
The Interchange
  Ind Est. PE29 — 6 C2
The Meadow Business
  Centre. PE27 — 13 E6
Ingram St. PE29 — 3 C2
Ivelbury Ct. PE19 — 18 B5

Keln Leas. PE27 — 13 D6
Kendall Way. PE28 — 10 B1
Kent Clo. PE27 — 12 C1
Kent Rd. PE29 — 7 E2
Kestrel Clo,
  Hartford. PE29 — 7 G2
Kestrel Clo,
  St Ives. PE27 — 12 B2
Kiln Clo. PE27 — 12 B3
King George Ct. PE19 — 18 B5
Kingfisher Gro. PE27 — 12 C2
Kingfisher Way. PE29 — 6 A4
Kings Clo. PE28 — 7 F2
Kings Gdns. PE29 — 6 D5
*Kings Hall, St Ives
  Business Pk. PE27 — 12 F4
Kings Hedges. PE27 — 12 C3
Kings Ripton Rd. PE28 — 6 D1
Kings Rd. PE27 — 13 D5
Kingsbrook. PE27 — 12 D3
Kisby Av. PE29 — 9 E2
Kite Clo. PE29 — 7 G2
Knipe Clo. PE29 — 6 B3
Knowles Clo. PE28 — 8 D3
Kyle Cres. PE28 — 8 C3

Lake Way. PE29 — 6 C4
Lakeview Ct. PE29 — 6 C2
Lammas Gdns. PE29 — 6 D5
Lammas Way. PE27 — 12 C4
Lamport Dri. PE27 — 7 F1
Lancaster Dri. PE27 — 12 C2
Lancaster Rd. PE28 — 10 B1
Lancaster Way,
  Godmanchester. PE29 — 9 D2
Lancaster Way,
  Huntingdon. PE29 — 6 B2
Lancelot Way. PE28 — 18 C2
Landcliffe Clo. PE27 — 12 D3
Langley Clo. PE27 — 12 C4
Langley Ct. PE27 — 12 C4
Langley Way. PE29 — 11 D3
Lark Cres. PE29 — 7 G4
Lark End. PE19 — 18 C5
Lark Way. PE29 — 4 C6
Laroc Ct. PE29 — 9 C3
Latham Rd. PE29 — 6 C2
Laughtons La. PE28 — 10 B5
Laurel Ct. PE29 — 3 A2
Lavender Ct. PE29 — 7 F2
Lavender Way. PE27 — 12 D3
Laws Cres. PE28 — 8 A2
Laxton Grange. PE28 — 19 B3
Layton Cres. PE28 — 8 B3
Lea Rd. PE28 — 11 E2
Leadens La. PE19 — 18 D6
Leechcroft. PE28 — 18 C2
Leger Ct. PE27 — 12 C3
Legion Way. PE29 — 9 E3
Lenton Clo. PE28 — 8 C4
Levers Water. PE29 — 6 B3
Lilac Way. PE27 — 12 D3
Lime Park Rd. PE27 — 13 C7
Limes Ct. PE27 — 13 C7
Lincoln Av. PE27 — 12 C2
Lincoln Clo. PE19 — 18 B4

Linden Gro. PE29 — 9 C2
Lindeth Clo. PE29 — 6 B3
Lingmoor. PE29 — 6 B4
Link Dri. PE28 — 8 A2
Links Way. PE27 — 12 C4
Linsay Clo. PE28 — 10 B1
Lions Cross. PE29 — 9 D3
Lions Yd. PE19 — 18 B5
Literary Wk. PE29 — 3 C2
Little Farthing Clo. PE27 — 13 E5
Little How. PE27 — 12 B2
Little Moor. PE28 — 18 C2
Littlefield Clo. PE29 — 9 D3
Lodge Clo. PE29 — 6 C6
Lomax Dri. PE28 — 8 B2
London Rd,
  Godmanchester. PE29 — 9 D3
London Rd,
  St Ives. PE27 — 13 C7
London St. PE29 — 9 C3
Long La. PE28 — 11 E3
Longstaff Way. PE29 — 7 G4
Lorna Ct. PE27 — 12 B2
Loughrigg Clo. PE29 — 6 B3
Love La. PE28 — 10 B5
Low Rd,
  Fenstanton. PE28 — 18 B1
Low Rd,
  Little Stukeley. PE28 — 5 G6
Low Rd, St Ives. PE27 — 13 C7
Loweswater. PE29 — 6 C5
Lowry Clo. PE28 — 12 D2
Loxley Grn. PE28 — 10 A5
Lucas Ct. PE29 — 7 F3
Lucks La. PE19 — 18 B5
Lysander Clo. PE27 — 12 C2

Macbeth Clo. PE29 — 7 F3
Madeley Ct. PE28 — 11 E2
Main St. PE29 — 7 G4
Malecoff. PE28 — 9 C4
Malthouse Clo. PE29 — 3 C3
Manchester Pl. PE29 — 3 B2
Manchester Rd. PE28 — 8 C5
Manchester Way. PE27 — 12 C1
Mandeville Rd. PE28 — 8 B3
Manor Clo,
  Brampton. PE28 — 8 D4
Manor Clo,
  Buckden. PE19 — 18 B5
Manor Clo,
  Wyton. PE28 — 10 A4
Manor Dri. PE28 — 18 B1
Manor Gdns. PE19 — 18 B5
Manor La. PE28 — 4 C4
Manor Mews. PE27 — 13 D5
Manor Rd. PE28 — 11 D2
Maple Clo,
  Huntingdon. PE29 — 7 E2
Maple Dri,
  Little Stukeley. PE28 — 5 H6
Maple End. PE28 — 4 C5
Margarets Way. PE29 — 6 C3
Margetts. PE28 — 11 F3
Market Hill,
  Huntingdon. PE29 — 3 B2
Market Hill,
  St Ives. PE27 — 13 D5
*Market La,
  Market Hill. PE27 — 13 D5
Market Rd. PE27 — 13 D5
Marlborough Clo. PE27 — 12 C2
Marley Rd. PE27 — 12 B1
Marsh La. PE28 — 11 E3
Martin Clo. PE29 — 9 D4
Maryland Av. PE29 — 7 F2
Maule Clo. PE29 — 7 E4
Mayfield. PE19 — 18 B5
Mayfield Cres. PE29 — 7 F4
Mayfield Rd. PE29 — 7 F4
Maytrees. PE27 — 13 C7
Meadow Clo,
  Hemingford Grey.
  PE28 — 11 E1
Meadow Clo,
  St Ives. PE27 — 13 E5
Meadow Drove. PE28 — 19 F2
Meadow How. PE27 — 12 B2
Meadow La,
  Earith. PE28 — 19 E3
Meadow La,
  Hemingford Abbots.
  PE28 — 11 B1

Meadow La,
  Hemingford Grey.
  PE28 — 11 E1
Meadow La,
  Houghton. PE28 — 10 B4
Meadow La,
  St Ives. PE27 — 13 D5
Meadow Way,
  Earith. PE28 — 19 F3
Meadow Way,
  Godmanchester. PE29 — 9 D2
Medway Rd. PE29 — 7 E3
Meeting Wk. PE28 — 19 B4
Megs Clo. PE28 — 19 B4
Mere Way. PE28 — 10 B4
Merlin Clo. PE29 — 7 G3
Merritt St. PE29 — 6 D5
Merryland. PE27 — 13 D5
Merton Wk. PE28 — 9 D3
Michigan Rd. PE28 — 12 B3
Middlemiss Vw. PE29 — 9 C4
Midgehall Ct. PE29 — 6 C2
Mill Clo, Hartford. PE29 — 7 G3
Mill Clo, Hemingford
  Grey. PE28 — 11 E2
Mill Clo,
  Little Stukeley. PE28 — 5 G6
Mill Common. PE29 — 3 B3
Mill La,
  Bluntisham. PE28 — 19 B3
Mill La, Hemingford
  Grey. PE28 — 11 E2
Mill Rd, Alconbury. PE28 — 4 C5
Mill Rd Buckden. PE19 — 18 C5
Mill Rd,
  Fen Drayton. CB4 — 18 D3
Mill Rd. Hartford. PE29 — 7 G4
Mill Rd,
  Little Stukeley. PE28 — 5 G6
Mill St. PE28 — 10 B5
Miller Clo. PE29 — 9 C4
Miller Way. PE28 — 8 B2
Millfield Ct. PE29 — 3 A2
Millside. PE27 — 13 D6
Milton Clo,
  Huntingdon. PE29 — 7 E3
Milton Clo,
  St Ives. PE27 — 12 C2
Mitchell Clo. PE28 — 11 E3
Moats Way. PE28 — 11 A4
Monet Clo. PE27 — 12 D1
Monks Cotts. PE19 — 18 C5
Montagu Rd. PE28 — 3 D2
Montague Rd. PE28 — 8 B5
Moorhouse Dri. PE29 — 7 E3
Morland Way. PE27 — 12 C1
Morris Clo. PE19 — 18 B6
Mowlands. PE29 — 6 D5
Mulberry Clo. PE28 — 6 D5
Myrtle Way. PE27 — 12 D4

Needingworth Rd. PE27 — 12 E4
Nelson Rd. PE29 — 7 F4
Nene Rd. PE29 — 7 E2
Nene Way. PE27 — 12 D2
New Rd,
  Hemingford Abbots.
  PE28 — 11 B4
New Rd, St Ives. PE27 — 13 D6
New St. PE29 — 9 C2
*Newham Hall, St Ives
  Business Pk. PE27 — 12 F4
Newman Ct. PE28 — 11 E3
Newnham Clo. PE29 — 7 F3
Newtons Ct. PE29 — 3 C2
Nicholas La. PE27 — 13 C5
Nightingale La. PE29 — 7 G4
Nimrod Dri. PE28 — 10 B1
Norfolk Rd,
  Huntingdon. PE29 — 7 E2
Norfolk Rd,
  St Ives. PE27 — 12 C1
Norfolk Rd,
  Wyton. PE28 — 10 C1
Norman Ct. PE28 — 11 D2
Norris Rd. PE27 — 13 D5
North Rd,
  Alconbury Weston.
  PE28 — 4 B4
North Rd,
  Brampton. PE28 — 8 C4
North Rd, St Ives. PE27 — 13 C5
North Side. PE28 — 6 D4
North St. PE29 — 7 E5
Nuffield Rd. PE27 — 12 E3

Nursery Gdns. PE27 12 E4
Nursery Rd. PE29 3 C1
Nursery Walk. PE28 8 B2

Oak Dri. PE28 8 B2
Oak End. PE28 4 C5
Oak Tree Clo. PE27 12 C3
Oak Tree Ct. PE29 7 G3
Oakfields. PE28 11 D2
Oaklands. PE28 18 C2
Oakleigh Cres. PE29 9 C3
Oberon Clo. PE29 7 G3
Old Church La. PE28 19 B1
Old Court Hall. PE29 9 C3
Old Farm Ct. PE28 19 A3
Old Glebe. PE28 4 C4
Old Houghton Rd. PE29 7 H4
Old Pound Clo. PE28 11 F2
Old Ramsey Rd. PE27 12 B1
Oliver Rd. PE27 13 D5
Olivia Rd. PE28 8 B3
Orchard Cres. PE28 19 E3
Orchard End. PE28 19 B4
Orchard Gdns. PE28 18 B2
Orchard La, Brampton. PE28 8 C3
Orchard La, Huntingdon. PE29 3 D3
Orchard Ter. PE27 13 D5
Orchard Way. PE29 9 C2
Oriel Ct. PE27 13 D5
Orthwaite. PE29 6 B4
Orwell Clo. PE27 12 D2
Osier Holt. PE28 19 C1
Osprey Clo. PE29 7 G2
Othello Clo. PE29 7 F3
Ouse Rd. PE27 12 D2
Ouse Wk. PE29 3 D2
Overwater Ct. PE29 6 A3
Owl Way. PE29 7 G3
Oxford Rd. PE27 13 D5
Oxmoor La. PE29 7 E4

Pages Way. PE28 8 B2
Palmers La. PE28 4 C6
Paragon Rd. PE27 12 C4
Parcell Wk. PE29 9 C4
Park Av. PE27 13 D5
Park End. PE19 18 C5
Park La, Brampton. PE28 8 B5
Park La, Godmanchester. PE29 9 C2
Park Rd, Brampton. PE28 8 B4
Park Rd, Buckden. PE19 18 C5
Park Rd, St Ives. PE27 13 E5
Parkgate. PE29 6 C4
Park View. PE28 6 A1
Parkside, Huntingdon. PE29 3 C1
Parkside, St Ives. PE27 13 D5
Parkway, Huntingdon. PE29 6 A5
Parkway, St Ives. PE27 12 D4
Parrens Rd. PE28 19 E3
Parsons Drove. PE27 12 F4
Parsons Grn. PE27 12 F4
Pathfinder Way. PE28 10 B1
Pavilion Clo. PE29 9 C2
Payne Clo. PE28 11 E3
Peaks Ct. PE29 6 B5
Pear Tree Clo. PE28 18 A3
Peate Clo. PE29 9 D3
Pembroke Clo, Hartford. PE29 7 F3
Pembroke Clo, St Ives. PE27 13 B6
*Pembroke Hall, St Ives Business Pk. PE27 12 F4
Pennington Rd. PE29 7 F2
Pepys Rd. PE28 8 D3
Peregrine Clo. PE29 7 G2
Perry Rd. PE18 18 A5
*Peterhouse Hall, St Ives Business Pk. PE27 12 F4
Pettis Rd. PE27 12 B2
Pettis Wk. PE27 12 B2
Pettit Clo. PE29 9 E3
Pig La. PE27 12 D4
Pinder Clo. PE29 9 D4
Pinfold La. PE29 9 C3
Pipers La. PE28 8 B2
Pitfield Clo. PE29 18 C2
Polecat La. PE28 4 B4

Pond Clo. PE29 6 A5
Poplar Clo. PE29 7 E3
Porch Clo. PE29 9 C3
Post St. PE29 9 C2
Pound Rd. PE28 11 E3
Presses Clo. PE28 19 B3
Primrose La. PE29 3 D1
Princes St. PE29 3 B2
Pringle Ct. PE28 5 G5
Pringle Way. PE28 5 G5
Priors Rd. PE28 11 D3
Priory Gro. PE28 3 C1
Priory La. PE29 7 E4
Priory Rd, Huntingdon. PE29 3 C1
Priory Rd, St Ives. PE27 13 D6
Prospero Way. PE29 7 F3
Provence Rd. PE29 6 B3

*Quay Ct, The Quay. PE27 13 D6
Queens Clo. PE27 12 D4
Queens Dri. PE29 7 F5

Ramsey Rd. PE27 12 B1
Ravenshoe. PE29 9 E3
Rectory Clo. PE29 8 D3
Rectory Gdns. PE28 9 D2
Rectory La. PE28 10 A5
Rectory Rd. PE28 19 B4
Red Bar. PE28 11 E3
Red Lion Clo. PE28 4 C5
Redmoor Clo. PE27 12 D2
Redwell Clo. PE27 12 B3
Redwongs Way. PE29 6 D3
Rembrandt Way. PE27 12 C1
Renoir Clo. PE27 12 C2
Renton Ct. PE29 3 D3
Reynolds Clo. PE27 12 C2
Rhymers Gate. PE29 10 A5
Ribble Clo. PE27 12 D2
Richmond Clo. PE29 7 E1
Riddiford Cres. PE28 8 B3
Rideaway. PE28 11 B1
Rideaway Dri. PE28 11 B2
River La. PE28 8 D5
River Meadow. PE28 11 B1
*Rivermill House, Enderbys Wharf. PE27 13 D5
Riverside Rd. PE29 3 D3
Robbs Wk. PE27 13 D5
Robin Ter. PE28 4 C5
Rodney Rd. PE29 7 F4
Roman Way. PE29 9 D4
Romney Clo. PE27 12 C2
Rookery Clo. PE27 12 E4
Rookery Pl. PE28 18 C2
Rookery Way. PE28 18 C2
Roscrea Ct. PE29 3 A2
Roscrea Ter. PE29 3 A2
Rosenthall Ter. PE28 11 E2
Rowan Clo. PE29 6 D5
Royal Oak La. PE28 11 B1
Royal Oak Pass. PE28 3 B2
Rubens Way. PE27 12 C2
Rushes Wk. PE29 9 D3
Rushington Clo. PE27 12 E3
Russett Clo. PE27 12 E3
Rusts La. PE28 4 C5
Rutland Clo. PE27 12 C1
Rydal Clo. PE29 6 C4

Saddlers Way. PE28 11 F3
*St Anns Ct, St Anns La. PE29 9 C2
St Anns La. PE29 9 C2
St Audrey Clo. PE27 12 E4
St Audrey La. PE27 12 D4
St Barnabas Ct. PE29 7 F3
St Benedicts Ct. PE29 3 C2
*St Catherines Hall, St Ives Business Pk. PE27 12 F4
St Clements Pass. PE29 3 C3
St Georges Clo. PE28 8 D4
St Georges Clo. PE29 3 B2
St Georges Rd. PE27 13 C5
St Germain St. PE29 3 C2
St Germain Wk. PE29 3 C2
St Hughs Rd. PE19 18 B4
St Ives Rd, Hemingford Grey. PE28 11 E2
St Ives Rd, Houghton. PE28 10 B5
St James Ct. PE28 11 E2

*St Johns Hall, St Ives Business Pk. PE27 12 F4
St Johns Rd. PE27 13 D5
St Johns St. PE29 3 A1
St Johns Ter. PE29 6 D5
St Margarets Rd. PE28 10 A4
St Marys. PE28 19 F2
St Marys Clo. PE28 19 B4
St Marys Clo. PE29 3 C3
St Marys Rd. PE28 19 B3
St Marys St. PE29 3 C3
St Peters Rd. PE29 6 D3
Salisbury Clo. PE27 12 C1
Sallowbush Rd. PE29 7 E3
Sallows. PE28 18 C1
Salon Way. PE29 6 B3
Sandwich Clo, Huntingdon. PE29 7 E3
Sandwich Clo, St Ives. PE27 12 C1
Sandwich Rd. PE28 8 B4
Sapley Pk. PE29 7 F2
Sapley Rd. PE29 7 F1
Sapley Sq. PE29 7 E2
Saunders Clo, Huntingdon. PE29 7 E3
Saunders Clo, Little Stukeley. PE28 5 G6
Sawtry Way. PE28 10 A1
Saxon Clo. PE29 9 C3
Sayer St. PE29 6 D5
Sayers Ct. PE28 19 B3
Scholars Av. PE29 6 C6
School La, Alconbury. PE28 4 C4
School La, Buckden. PE19 18 C4
School La, Fenstanton. PE28 18 C1
School La, Hartford. PE29 7 G4
School Rd. PE28 19 E3
Scorney. PE28 18 C1
Scrolans. PE27 12 B2
Sears Clo. PE29 9 C3
Seathwaite. PE29 6 B4
Second Drove. PE29 13 E6
Selby St. PE29 7 F2
*Selwyn Hall, St Ives Business Pk. PE27 12 F4
Shakespeare Rd. PE27 12 B3
Sharp Clo. PE27 12 B3
Sharps La. PE28 4 C6
Sheepfold. PE27 12 E4
Shelley Clo. PE29 7 F3
Short Drove. PE28 19 F2
Short La. PE28 19 A3
*Sidney Sussex Hall, St Ives Business Pk. PE27 12 F4
Silver Birch Av. PE27 12 C2
Silver Birch Clo. PE29 7 E3
Silver St, Buckden. PE19 18 B4
Silver St, Godmanchester. PE29 9 C3
Simmer Piece. PE28 18 C2
Skeels Clo. PE29 7 F2
Skeggles Clo. PE29. 6 C4
Skelton Pl. PE28 12 D3
Sleepe Clo. PE27 13 D5
Smith Dri. PE19 18 C6
Snowdonia Way. PE29 6 B6
Snowy Way. PE29 7 H3
Sokemans Way. PE28 8 B6
Somerset Rd. PE28 10 C2
Somersham Rd. PE27 12 E2
South Rd. PE28 8 C5
South Side. PE29 6 D4
South St. PE29 7 F5
Sparrow Clo, Brampton. PE28 8 B6
Sparrow Clo, Huntingdon. PE29 7 E4
Sparrow Dri. PE28 4 C6
Sparrowhawk Way. PE29 7 G3
Spencer Dri. PE27 12 C2
Spinney Clo. PE28 8 C3
Spinney La. PE28 4 C5
Spinney Way. PE27 12 C3
Spires End. PE28 4 B3
Spitfire Clo. PE29 6 B2
Spittals Way. PE29 6 C3
Splash La. PE28 10 A4
Spring Clo. PE29 7 E3
Springfield Clo. PE29 7 E4

Springfield Clo. PE19 18 B6
Springfield Rd. PE28 4 A4
Stanpoint Way. PE27 12 D4
Stanton Way. PE29 6 C4
Starling Clo. PE28 4 C6
Station Rd, Bluntisham. PE28 19 A4
Station Rd, St Ives. PE27 13 D6
Stephenson Rd. PE27 12 E2
Stepping Stones. PE28 11 F3
Stewart Clo. PE28 8 A3
Stickle Clo. PE29 6 B3
Stirling Rd. PE27 12 C2
Stirtloe La. PE19 18 B6
Stocks Bridge Way. PE27 12 F4
Stonehill. PE29 6 C3
Stoney Clo. PE29 7 F2
Stour Clo. PE27 12 D2
Stuart Clo. PE29 9 D3
Stubbs Clo. PE27 12 C2
Stukeley Rd. PE29 6 C3
Suffolk Clo, Huntingdon. PE29 7 F4
Suffolk Clo, St Ives. PE27 12 C1
Sumerling Way. PE28 19 B3
Surrey Rd. PE29 7 E2
Sussex Rd. PE28 10 B1
Swan Clo. PE27 12 B2
Swan End. PE19 18 C5
Swan Gdns. PE28 18 C2
Sweetings Rd. PE29 9 C3
Sycamore Dri. PE29 7 E2
Sylton Clo. PE29 9 D2

Talls La. PE28 18 C1
Tamar Clo. PE27 12 D3
Tanglewood. PE28 4 B3
*Tanners Quay, Wellington St. PE27 13 D6
Tawny Cres. PE29 7 H3
Tay Clo. PE27 12 E2
Taylors La. PE19 18 B4
Teal Clo. PE27 12 B2
Temple Clo. PE29 3 D3
Tennis Court Av. PE29 3 D1
Tennyson Av. PE27 12 B2
Tennyson Clo. PE29 7 F4
Tenterleas. PE27 13 D5
Thackray Clo. PE29 7 E3
Thames Rd. PE29 7 F2
The Acre. PE28 4 C5
The Apple Orchard. PE28 11 F2
The Avenue. PE29 9 C1
The Barns. PE19 18 C5
The Brambles. PE27 13 B7
The Broadway. PE27 13 D5
The Brow. PE29 3 D2
The Chestnuts. PE29 9 C3
The Close. PE29 9 D3
The Crescent. PE29 12 C3
The Drive. PE27 13 C5
The Fairway. PE29 19 A3
The Fen. PE28 18 C1
The Furrows. PE28 12 D4
The Gables. PE28 18 B2
The Green, Brampton. PE28 8 B3
The Green, Houghton. PE28 10 B5
The Grove, Buckden. PE19 18 B5
The Grove, Huntingdon. PE29 7 H4
The Hawthorns. P28 19 A3
The Hollow. PE28 10 B5
The Lanes. PE28 10 B5
The Leys. PE28 4 C6
The Mallards. PE27 13 B6
The Maltings, Alconbury. PE28 4 C4
The Maltings, Godmanchester. PE29 9 C3
The Maltsters. PE19 18 B5
The Mill. PE29 13 D6
The Oaks. PE28 10 A5
The Orchards. PE28 10 A5
The Osiers. PE19 18 B6
The Paddock, Bluntisham. PE28 19 A3
The Paddock, Huntingdon. PE29 7 E5
The Paddocks. PE28 4 C4

*The Pavement, Market Hill. PE27 13 D5
The Poplars. PE29 19 A3
The Pound. PE27 12 D3
The Quadrant. PE27 13 D5
The Quay. PE27 13 D6
The Rampleys. PE28 11 F2
The Rhees. PE28 19 B2
The Ridings. PE27 13 D6
The Shires. PE28 19 A4
The Spinney. PE29 7 G4
The Stiles. PE29 9 C2
The Sycamores. PE28 19 A3
The Thicket. PE29 6 B4
The Thorpe. PE28 11 D2
The Views. PE29 3 B2
The Vineyards. PE28 19 B1
The Waits. PE27 13 C5
The Walks North. PE29 3 B3
The Waterhaven. PE28 19 E4
The Whaddons. PE29 7 F3
The Whistlers. PE27 12 D2
The Wilderness. PE27 13 C6
Thicket Rd. PE28 10 B5
Thickwillow. PE29 9 D4
Thirlmere. PE29 6 B4
Thomas King Dri. PE29 6 C4
Thongsley. PE29 7 F3
Thorndown Clo. PE27 12 B2
Thrapston Rd. PE28 8 B2
Throckmorton Dri. PE28 8 B6
Tomlinson Ct. PE29 7 F2
Tower Clo. PE29 6 D1
Towerfield. PE28 7 E1
Townsend Clo. PE28 10 A4
Trent Clo. PE27 12 D2
Trinity Pl PE29 3 C2
Tudor Rd. PE29 9 D2
Turberville Ct. PE28 11 D3
Turner Rd. PE27 12 D1
Tythe Piece. PE29 18 C2

Ullswater. PE29 6 C5

Valiant Rd. PE27 12 C2
Van Dyke Pl. PE27 12 C2
Van Gogh Pl. PE27 12 C2
Veasey Rd. PE29 7 F3
Vermuyden. PE28 19 F3
Vicarage Flds. PE28 11 E2
Victor Clo. PE27 12 C2
Victor St. PE28 10 B1
Victoria Cres. PE28 10 B5
Victoria Sq. PE29 3 D2
Victoria Ter. PE27 13 C6
Vine Clo. PE27 13 B6
Vinegar Hill. PE28 4 B3
Vineyard Way. PE19 18 C5
Virginia Way. PE27 12 B3

Walden Gro. PE29 3 B3
Walden Rd. PE29 3 B2
Wallace Ct. PE29 7 G2
Walnut Tree Gro. PE29 8 C3
Walnut Tree Dri. PE29 6 D4
Walnut Tree Cres. PE28 18 C2
Ward Clo. PE28 10 B5
Ware La. PE28 10 A5
Warners Gro. PE27 12 D4
Warren Clo. PE28 10 A4
Warren Ct. PE27 12 E4
Warren Rd. PE27 12 D4
Washingley Rd. PE29 6 C2
Wastwater. PE29 6 B4
Waterloo Clo. PE28 8 B3
Watts La. PE28 11 C4
Waveney Rd. PE27 12 D2
Weir Clo, Buckden. PE19 18 B4
Weir Clo, Hemingford. PE29 11 E1
Weir Rd. PE28 11 E2
Welland Clo. PE27 12 D2
Wellington Av, St Ives. PE27 12 C4
Wellington Av, Wyton. PE28 10 B5
Wellington St. PE27 13 D6
Wells Clo. PE28 8 B2
Wellsfield. PE28 7 E1
Wensum Clo. PE27 12 D2
Wertheim Way. PE29 6 B1
Wessell. PE28 10 B5
West Clo. PE28 4 A4
West End. PE28 8 A4

West End Rd. PE28 18 A2
West Leys. PE27 12 C4
West Side. PE29 6 D4
West St,
Godmanchester. PE29 9 B3
West St,
Huntingdon. PE29 7 E5
West St, St Ives. PE27 13 C5
Westbrook Clo. PE28 8 A2
Westbury Rd. PE27 12 C4
Westmeare. PE28 11 D2
Westmorland Av. PE28 10 B2
Westwood Clo. PE27 13 C5
Westwood Rd. PE27 12 C4
Wheatfields. PE27 12 C3
Wheatley Cres. PE28 19 A3
Wheatsheaf Rd. PE28 4 A4
Whinfell Clo. PE29 6 B3
*White Hart La,
White Hart La. PE27 13 D5
White Hart La,
Godmanchester. PE29 9 D3
White Hart La,
St Ives. PE27 13 D5
Whitecross. PE27 12 C4
Wigmore Clo. PE29 9 C3
Williams Clo. PE28 8 A3
Willow Clo. PE28 8 B3
Willow End. PE28 4 C5
Willow Farm Clo. PE28 4 A3
Willow Way. PE27 12 E4
Wilson Way. PE28 8 C5
Wiltshire Rd. PE28 10 C1
Windermere. PE28 6 C4
Windover Rd. PE29 6 D3
Windsor Clo. PE27 12 C1
Windsor Rd. PE29 9 D3
Witham Clo. PE27 12 D2
Wood End. PE28 19 A3
Wood St. PE29 3 C2
Wood Vw. PE28 8 A2
Woodley Ct. PE29 9 C2
Woodside Way. PE27 12 D4
Woolley Rd. PE28 8 B2
Woolpack La. PE27 13 D5
Wren Clo. PE28 4 C6

Yellowgate Rd. PE28 10 B1
York Clo. PE29 9 D2
York Rd. PE28 10 B2
York Sq. PE28 10 B2
York Way. PE27 12 C1

ST. NEOTS

Acacia Gro. PE19 15 G6
Ackerman Gdns. PE19 16 C4
Ackerman St. PE19 16 B4
Addington Wk. PE19 16 C4
Admirals Way. PE19 16 A4
Alamein Ct. PE19 16 C1
Alder Clo. PE19 14 B6
Alington Rd. PE19 17 F5
Almond Rd. PE19 15 F6
Alnwick Ct. PE19 17 E3
Andrew Rd. PE19 17 E4
Anson Pl. PE19 16 A3
Apple Grn. PE19 16 C2
Appleby Ct. PE19 3 B4
Arnhem Clo. PE19 16 C1
Arundel Cres. PE19 17 E4
Audrey Ct. PE19 16 B3
Avon Ct. PE19 3 C4
Axis Way. PE19 16 B1

Balmoral Way. PE19 17 E4
Barford Rd. PE19 16 D1
Barker Clo. PE19 14 A3
Barley La. PE19 16 D1
Barley Rd. PE19 16 C2
Barnard Clo. PE19 17 E4
Barnes Clo. PE19 15 E6
Baron Pl. PE19 16 B2
Barringer Way. PE19 15 G6
Bean Clo. PE19 15 G6
Beatty Rd. PE19 16 B3
Beauchamp Clo. PE19 16 B3
Beaver Clo. PE19 16 B2
Bec Clo. PE19 3 B5
Bedford St. PE19 3 B4
Beech Gro. PE19 15 E6
Beech Ho,
Howitts La. PE19 17 E2

Beeson Clo. PE19 15 F2
Beezling Clo. PE19 14 C6
Begwary Clo. PE19 16 B1
Berkley Ct. PE19 3 B6
Berkley St. PE19 17 E2
Berkley Ter. PE19 17 E3
Bilberry Clo. PE19 14 C6
Bird La. PE19 14 A3
Bishops Rd. PE19 17 E4
Blackwood Rd. PE19 16 B3
Blair Way. PE19 17 E4
Blakes Way. PE19 16 B3
Blenheim Clo. PE19 16 C1
Bloomfield Clo. PE19 15 E3
Boardman Clo. PE19 15 F2
Bodiam Way. PE19 17 E4
Booth Way. PE19 15 F3
Bowers Mill. PE19 3 A6
Brampton Gdns. PE19 17 F2
*Brickhills,
Hen Brook. PE19 17 F2
*Brigade Ho, Alington Rd
Business Pk. PE19 17 E5
Brook Rd. PE19 16 C2
Brook St. PE19 3 B6
Browning Dri. PE19 14 C5
Browns Sq. PE19 3 D6
Buckley Rd. PE19 17 E2
Burns Clo. PE19 14 D6
Burnt Clo. PE19 17 E2
Burwell Rd. PE19 14 C6
Bushmead Gdns. PE19 15 F2
Bushmead Rd. PE19 16 A2
Bydand La. PE19 15 F2
Byng Clo. PE19 16 B3
Byron Pl. PE19 14 C6

Caernarvon Rd. PE19 17 E4
Caldecote Rd. PE19 17 E2
Cambridge Clo. PE19 3 C5
Cambridge Gdns. PE19 3 C5
Cambridge Rd. PE19 17 G1
Cambridge St. PE19 3 C5
Capulet Clo. PE19 16 C3
Carisbrooke Way. PE19 17 E4
Castle Hill Clo. PE19 16 C4
Cavendish Ct. PE19 16 D1
Cawdor Pl. PE19 17 E4
Cemetery Rd. PE19 3 C6
Chamberlain Way. PE19 15 F4
Chandlers Wharf. PE19 3 B6
Charles St. PE19 3 D6
Chaucer Pl. PE19 14 C6
Chawston Clo. PE19 16 B1
Chestnut Gro. PE19 17 E1
Childs Pond Rd. PE19 15 G6
Church Clo. PE19 15 F2
Church Meadows. PE19 3 C6
Church St. PE19 3 C6
Church Vw. PE19 3 C6
Church Wk. PE19 3 B5
Clover Rd. PE19 16 C2
Codrington Ct. PE19 16 B3
Coleridge Ct. PE19 14 C5
*Collingwood Ho, Alington Rd
Business Pk. PE19 17 E5
Collingwood Rd. PE19 16 B4
Colmworth Gdns. PE19 16 C4
Compton Clo. PE19 17 E4
Constable Av. PE19 14 C6
Conway Pl. PE19 17 E3
Corfe Pl. PE19 17 E3
Cornwall Clo. PE19 16 B1
Cornwallis Dri. PE19 16 A3
Corunna Clo. PE19 16 C1
Countess Clo. PE19 16 B2
Cowpers Ct. PE19 14 D6
Crecy Clo. PE19 16 C1
Cressener Ter. PE19 3 C5
Criccieth Way. PE19 17 E4
Cromwell Clo. PE19 17 F3
Cromwell Gdns. PE19 17 G1
Cromwell Rd. PE19 17 F2
Cross Keys Mall. PE19 3 A5
Crosshall Rd. PE19 14 C5
Crown Clo. PE19 14 A3
Crown Wk. PE19 16 B2
Culloden Clo. PE19 16 C1
Cumberland Way. PE19 17 F4
Curlew Pl. PE19 15 G5

Dairy Ct. PE19 3 C4
Darrington Clo. PE19 16 B3
Davis Clo. PE19 15 G2
Dew Pond Clo. PE19 15 G6
Dial Clo. PE19 15 F2

Digby Ct. PE19 16 B3
Dovehouse Clo. PE19 3 C4
Drake Rd. PE19 16 B4
Dryden Ct. PE19 3 D6
Duchess Clo. PE19 16 A2
Duck La. PE19 17 F1
Dukes Rd. PE19 16 B2
Duloe Rd. PE19 16 C1
Dunster Way. PE19 17 E4

Eagle Ct. PE19 15 H5
Earl Clo. PE19 16 B1
East Clo. PE19 3 C5
East St. PE19 3 C5
Eaton Ford Grn. PE19 16 D1
Eayre Ct. PE19 3 D6
Edinburgh Dri. PE19 16 B2
Edward Rd. PE19 17 F4
Elizabeth Ct. PE19 16 C1
Elm Croft. PE19 15 F1
*Elm Ho,
Howitts La. PE19 15 F5
Emery Pl. PE19 15 F5

Fairfax Ct. PE19 17 F2
Falcon Clo. PE19 15 G5
Fallow Dri. PE19 16 B1
Falstaff Rd. PE19 16 C3
Farcet Clo. PE19 14 C5
Ferrars Av. PE19 17 E2
Field Clo. PE19 15 F1
Field Cottage Rd. PE19 16 C2
Fielding Ct. PE19 14 C5
Fishers Yd. PE19 3 B6
Flint Way. PE19 16 C3
Ford Clo. PE19 16 D1
Forge Clo. PE19 16 B4
Foundry Way. PE19 16 B4
Fox Brook Ct. PE19 3 C5
Fox Clo. PE19 15 G6
Foxglove Clo. PE19 14 C6
Freemantle Ct. PE19 16 B3
Fydell Clo. PE19 15 G5

Gainsborough Av. PE19 14 C6
Gazelle Clo. PE19 16 B1
George Pl. PE19 17 F4
Gery Ct. PE19 16 B1
Glamis Ct. PE19 17 E4
Glenarrif. PE19 17 E2
Gordon Clo. PE19 15 F3
Gordon Rd. PE19 15 E3
Gorham Pl. PE19 16 D1
Great North Rd,
Eaton Ford. PE19 14 C6
Great North Rd,
Eaton Socon. PE19 16 B5
Great North Rd,
Little Paxton. PE19 15 E5
Grebe Way. PE19 15 G5
Green Gables. PE19 16 B1
Green End Rd. PE19 3 D5
Green La. PE19 14 A3
Greenfields. PE19 15 G6
Grenville Way. PE19 16 B4
Grosvenor Gdns. PE19 3 B4
Grove Ct. PE19 15 F1
Grove Rd. PE19 15 E1

Hall Clo. PE19 15 F1
Hall Rd. PE19 17 E3
Hampden Way. PE19 17 F3
Hanover Clo. PE19 16 D1
Hardwick Rd. PE19 17 E2
Hardy Pl. PE19 14 C5
Hargood Ct. PE19 16 B3
Harland Rd. PE19 15 E6
Harlech Ct. PE19 17 E3
Harvey St. PE19 17 E2
Hathaway Clo. PE19 16 B3
Hatley Clo. PE19 16 C3
Hawkesden Rd. PE19 15 G6
Hawkesford Way. PE19 15 F5
Hawthorn Clo. PE19 15 E1
Hawthorn Rd. PE19 15 E6
Hayling Av. PE19 15 F2
Hempsals. PE19 14 C6
Hen Brook. PE19 17 F2
Heron Ct. PE19 15 G5
High St,
Hail Weston. PE19 14 A3
High St,
Little Paxton. PE19 15 E2
High St, St Neots. PE19 3 B5
Hill Rise. PE19 15 G6
Hogarth Pl. PE19 14 C6

Honeydon Av. PE19 16 B1
Howard Rd. PE19 16 B5
Howitts Gdns. PE19 17 F4
Howitts La. PE19 17 F2
Humberley Clo. PE19 17 E3
Huntingdon Rd. PE19 15 F5
Huntingdon St. PE19 3 C5
*Hydropore Ho, Alington Rd
Business Pk. PE19 17 E5

INDUSTRIAL & RETAIL:
Admiral Ct
Business Pk. PE19 17 E5
Alington Rd
Business Pk. PE19 17 E5
Colmworth Business Pk.
PE19 16 C5
Howard Rd Ind Est.
PE19 16 C4
Ingles Ct. PE19 3 C4
Inkerman Rise. PE19 16 C1
Ireton Clo. PE19 17 F2
Ivel Clo. PE19 16 C2

James Ct. PE19 17 F4
Jellicoe Pl. PE19 16 A3
Jenkins Clo. PE19 16 A3
*Jimea Ho, Alington Rd
Business Pk. PE19 17 E5
Jubilee Clo. PE19 15 F2
Jutland Rise. PE19 16 C1

Keats Ct. PE19 14 C6
Kenilworth Clo. PE19 16 C3
*Keppal Ho, Alington Rd
Business Pk. PE19 17 E5
Kestrel Pl. PE19 15 G5
Kimbolton Rd. PE19 14 A3
Kingfisher Clo. PE19 15 G2
Kings La. PE19 3 D4
Kings Rd,
Eaton Socon. PE19 16 B2
Kings Rd,
St Neots. PE19 3 D4
Kipling Ct. PE19 14 D6
Knaresborough Ct. PE19 17 F5
Knights Clo. PE19 16 B2
Kym Rd. PE19 16 C2

Lady Way. PE19 16 B1
Lakefield Av. PE19 15 F2
Lakeside Clo. PE19 15 F2
Lammas Way. PE19 15 E6
Langwood Clo. PE19 14 C6
Lansbury Clo. PE19 17 E2
Laurel Clo. PE19 17 F2
Lawrence Rd. PE19 16 C1
Laxton Clo. PE19 16 C1
Lee Ct. PE19 3 B6
Levellers La. PE19 17 F3
Leys Rd. PE19 15 E6
Lime Gro. PE19 15 E6
Linclare Pl. PE19 16 C2
Lindisfarne Clo. PE19 17 F5
Linley Rd. PE19 17 E2
Little End Rd. PE19 16 B4
Little Paxton La. PE19 15 E2
Longfellow Pl. PE19 16 D1
Longsands Rd. PE19 15 G6
Lottings Way. PE19 14 C6
Lowry Rd. PE19 14 C6
Luke St. PE19 17 E2

*Maddison Ho,
Bedford St. PE19 3 B4
*Malden Ho,
Bedford St. PE19 3 B4
Mallard La. PE19 3 D6
Manor Clo. PE19 15 E2
Manor Farm Rd. PE19 17 G1
Manor Gro. PE19 17 F1
Manor Ho Clo. PE19 16 B3
Manor Pk. PE19 17 F1
Manor Way. PE19 14 A3
Marchioness Way. PE19 16 B2
*Marina Heights,
South St. PE19 3 B6
Market Sq. PE19 3 A5
Marlowe Ct. PE19 14 D5
Marquis Clo. PE19 16 B2
Marshall Rd. PE19 3 D6
Marston Rd. PE19 17 F2
Masefield Clo. PE19 14 C6
Meadow Clo,
Little Paxton. PE19 15 E2

Meadow Clo,
St Neots. PE19 3 C6
Meadowsweet. PE19 14 B6
Medallion Ct. PE19 3 C5
Medland Gro. PE19 3 D6
Merlin Clo. PE19 15 H5
Mill Hill Rd. PE19 16 C1
Mill La. PE19 15 E3
Mill View Ct. PE19 16 C4
Milton Av. PE19 14 C5
Minden Clo. PE19 16 C1
Monarch Rd. PE19 16 A2
Montagu St. PE19 17 E2
Moores Wk. PE19 3 B5
Mountbatten Ct. PE19 16 C2
Mountfort Clo. PE19 17 E3
Mullien Clo. PE19 14 C6
Muntjac Clo. PE19 16 B1
Murrell Clo. PE19 15 F5
Murrell Ct. PE19 15 F5
Musgrave Way. PE19 3 D6

Naseby Gdns. PE19 17 F2
Navigation Wharf. PE19 3 B6
*Nelson Ho, Alington Rd
Business Pk. PE19 17 E5
Nelson Rd. PE19 16 B3
Nene Rd. PE19 16 C2
New St. PE19 3 B4
Newtown Rd. PE19 14 B3
Nightingale Way. PE19 15 H5
Northfield Rd. MK44 16 A5
Nursery Gdns. PE19 15 G1
Nursery Rd. PE19 15 F1

Oak Clo. PE19 15 G6
Ockenden Clo. PE19 16 B3
Old Bull Yd. PE19 3 B6
Old School Gdns. PE19 16 C4
Orchard Clo,
Eaton Ford. PE19 16 C1
Orchard Clo,
Hail Weston. PE19 14 A3
Orchard Clo. PE19 16 C1
Orchid Clo. PE19 14 C6
Osier Ct. PE19 14 C5
Otter Way. PE19 16 B1
Ouse Rd. PE19 16 C2

Paines Mill. PE19 3 B4
Park Av. PE19 15 E2
Park Clo. PE19 15 E2
Park Cres. PE19 15 E2
Park Dri. PE19 15 E3
Park Rd. PE19 15 F5
Park View Ct. PE19 16 D1
Parkside. PE19 15 E2
Parkway,
Little Paxton. PE19 15 E2
Parkway,
St Neots. PE19 15 F5
Paxton Ct. PE19 16 B1
Peer Rd. PE19 16 B1
Pembroke Av. PE19 17 E4
Penrwyn Ct. PE19 17 E4
*Peppercorn Ho,
New St. PE19 3 B5
Peppercorn La. PE19 3 B5
Pepys Rd. PE19 17 F1
Philip Gdns. PE19 17 F4
Phoenix Sq. PE19 3 B4
Pope Rd. PE19 17 E2
Popham Clo. PE19 16 A3
Potton Rd. PE19 17 F3
Pound Clo. PE19 14 B3
Powis Pl. PE19 17 E4
Prince Clo. PE19 16 B1
Princes Dri. PE19 3 D4
Priory Hill Rd. PE19 15 G4
Priory La. PE19 3 A5
Priory Mall. PE19 3 A5
Priory Row. PE19 3 A4
Prospect Row. PE19 3 C5
Pulleyn Ct. PE19 3 B5

Queens Ct. PE19 16 B2
Queens Gdns. PE19 16 B2
Queensway. PE19 15 E5

Raleigh Clo. PE19 16 A3
Rampley Clo. PE19 15 E3
Rampley La. PE19 15 E1
Raven Clo. PE19 15 G5
Redwing Pl. PE19 15 H5
Regent Clo. PE19 16 B2
Reynolds Ct. PE19 14 C6